Connecting the Dots Between
EDUCATION, INTERESTS, AND CAREERS
Grades 7–10

A Guide for School Practitioners

SARAH M. KLERK

CORWIN
A SAGE Company

CORWIN
A SAGE Company

FOR INFORMATION:

Corwin
A SAGE Company
2455 Teller Road
Thousand Oaks, California 91320
(800) 233-9936
www.corwin.com

SAGE Publications Ltd.
1 Oliver's Yard
55 City Road
London EC1Y 1SP
United Kingdom

SAGE Publications India Pvt. Ltd.
B 1/I 1 Mohan Cooperative Industrial Area
Mathura Road, New Delhi 110 044
India

SAGE Publications Asia-Pacific Pte. Ltd.
3 Church Street
#10-04 Samsung Hub
Singapore 049483

Acquisitions Editor: Jessica Allan
Associate Editor: Kimberly Greenberg
Editorial Assistant: Heidi Arndt
Production Editors: Cassandra Margaret Seibel and
                       Melanie Birdsall
Typesetter: C&M Digitals (P) Ltd.
Proofreader: Caryne Brown
Cover Designer: Rose Storey
Permissions Editor: Karen Ehrmann

Printed in the United States of America.

Library of Congress Cataloging-in-Publication Data

Klerk, Sarah M.
Connecting the dots between education, interests, and careers, grades 7–10 : a guide for school practitioners / Sarah M. Klerk.

pages cm
Includes bibliographical references.

ISBN 978-1-4522-7190-3 (pbk. : alk. paper)
1. Career education. 2. Vocational guidance. 3. Middle schools—Curricula. I. Title.

LC1037.K58 2013
370.113—dc23   2013002131

This book is printed on acid-free paper.

SUSTAINABLE FORESTRY INITIATIVE
Certified Chain of Custody
Promoting Sustainable Forestry
www.sfiprogram.org
SFI-01268

SFI label applies to text stock

13 14 15 16 17 10 9 8 7 6 5 4 3 2 1

TABLE OF CONTENTS

Access resources for *Connecting the Dots Between Education, Interests, and Careers, Grades 7–10* at www.corwin.com/connectingthedots.

INTRODUCTION

Connecting the Dots Between Education, Interests, and Careers, Grades 7–10: A Guide for School Practitioners expands student knowledge about college and careers, excites students about college and careers, and informs student and family decision making.

Connecting the Dots has been created at a point in our history when education and skills training beyond high school are increasingly necessary to meet the educational and skill requirements of many current and emerging careers. By 2018, 63 percent of job openings will require workers to have at least some college education.[1] Despite the fact that the labor market demands more educational attainment than ever before, public high school graduation rates are consistently low—the national graduation rate stands at 69 percent.[2] For African American and Hispanic public school students, about 45 percent fail to graduate on time.[3] *Connecting the Dots* has been designed to help students in grades 7–10 understand why education is necessary for their future success by connecting the dots among school, interests, abilities, training, college and careers—all through a fun fact-finding mission that challenges students with interesting questions linking education to future career success. It is a discussion tool that provides adults— teachers, educators, parents—with engaging questions to stimulate dialogue with students about staying in school and is delivered through an easy-to-use question/ answer format and includes visual aids for visual learners.

Every school day in America, public high schools lose more than 7,200 students or one student every 25 seconds.[4] Many of those who drop out before high school graduation are caught up in an inescapable world of poverty. High school drop-outs are more likely to be unemployed, earn lower wages, be involved in criminal activity, need public assistance, and be single parents.[5] The employment outlook for a high school dropout is employment that pays less than a living wage, and employment prospects do not improve with time. In fact, over the course of his or her lifetime, a high school dropout earns, on average, about $260,000 less than a high school graduate.[6] *Connecting the Dots* addresses these facts and incorporates information on training and educational requirements that match interests, abilities, and career aspirations, recognizing that college isn't the only avenue that individuals can take to become highly employable. It highlights why education is necessary and emphasizes the positive impact education has on students' lives if grades K–12 are used to prepare for college or a career.

Today's careers demand training beyond high school via technical schools, community or four-year colleges, or beyond. For many youth, the transition between school and work is difficult. The educational and workforce systems are not well aligned—making it hard for individuals to match career options with educational decisions. *Connecting the Dots* matches education, training, and careers to provide students with a tool kit that will help them navigate the world of work, which is a key to being successful in the labor market.

Connecting the Dots is designed to be an easy-to-use tool for adults that is also engaging and interesting for students; it includes 45 main talking points in a question/answer format; extension activities and supplemental discussion questions to encourage interaction and learning; and illustrations (e.g., tables, charts, and graphics) for visual learners. Many of the extension activities, supplemental discussions, and graphics can be downloaded and printed at **www.corwin.com/connectingthedots.** The icon to the left will identify materials throughout *Connecting the Dots* that can be downloaded and printed for students.

The more students hear and read facts about the advantage gained by attending college and preparing for a career, the more they will be prepared to pursue a career. The consistency of information will reinforce other positive peer/family/school information that students receive about going to college. With *Connecting the Dots*, we can help students realize that they are not simply scrambling to get their work in on time; together we are preparing students for their future.

Connecting the Dots is adaptable and can be used in a classroom, after-school program, and club or camp setting. It is intended to be a discussion stimulator for teachers, mentors, and families to incorporate into their existing schedules. Its question/answer format requires minimal planning or preparation on their part. The different topics were developed in collaboration with teachers and experts in workforce development to focus learning on critical subjects. The questions highlight the importance of education and its relationship to careers, and they generate inquiry, discussion, and constructive conversation. *Connecting the Dots* includes nine topics that begin with "Education: The Key to Your Future," progress through "Ready or Not: High School, Here We Come," and end with "College Life: Much More Than Studying and Classes, It's Fun!"

SUGGESTED USE

Connecting the Dots Between Education, Interests, and Careers, Grades 7–10 has been developed to fit into any classroom schedule, mentorship or after-school program. Each of the nine topics includes five main talking points (questions/answers) that will generate excitement and engage students in a fun way to help them focus on their future and embrace the connections among school, careers, and rewarding lives. The answers are provided in a summary format to help the facilitator quickly prepare for the conversation.

In schools, *Connecting the Dots* can be used for one week in each of the nine months of the academic year. Another strategy for using *Connecting the Dots* in schools is to present segments at the same time every week so that it becomes a part of the weekly agenda over the course of the year. *Connecting the Dots* is designed to easily meet your classroom schedule.

For mentors, *Connecting the Dots* can be used to start or end sessions with mentees. The questions are so easy to use that it will start or end your time together on a positive note and keep students thinking about their current and future success.

For families, *Connecting the Dots* can be used during any free moments. It can be used in the kitchen and around the breakfast table to remind students why they are going to school. It can be used on the bus or in the car while traveling. It can provide stimulating discussions at any "check-in" points throughout the day such as at the dinner table or while on the phone.

Connecting the Dots includes extension activities, supplemental discussion questions, career definitions, illustrations, and resources (published here and also downloadable at **www.corwin.com/connectingthedots**) to assist in deepening conversations and opportunities for learning. The order of topics (listed in the Table of Contents on page v) is suggested, but each school, mentorship, or after-school program has different needs, and in some cases, it may make sense to change the order depending on those needs.

DIRECTIONS

Connecting the Dots Between Education, Interests, and Careers, Grades 7–10 facilitators can easily deliver the daily message with minimal planning. To familiarize themselves with the content of each new topic, facilitators of *Connecting the Dots* should first read the topic introduction. Prior to each discussion, facilitators should read the question and potential answers to become familiar with the material covered. Last, if there is a graphic that is associated with the discussion question, go to the website **www.corwin.com/ connectingthedots,** find the graphic, download it, and print the graphic. That's all the preparation that is needed to prepare for a meaningful conversation with students. The facilitator should then read students the question and potential answers and have the students answer the question. The suggested answer to each question is highlighted, and a brief explanation of the suggested answer is provided. The facilitator then should read or paraphrase the summary and, time permitting, encourage brief discussion. Optional supplementary activities and discussion questions are offered and intended to encourage students to think more deeply and critically about the topic. Many of the questions are followed by talking points that have been incorporated to assist the conversation and for teachers/mentors/facilitators to prod the students and keep them on track.

ABOUT THE DATA[7]

Much of the data used in *Connecting the Dots Between Education, Interests, and Careers, Grades 7–10* have been retrieved from public sources such as the United States Bureau of Statistics' Occupational Employment Survey and Occupational Outlook Handbook. The data provided throughout this document represent a snapshot of the educational and labor market conditions in the United States for the time period 2000 to 2018. The facts in this document (e.g., wage data, cost of living estimates, job growth projections) may reasonably change over time.

Occupational Employment Survey: Wage data included in *Connecting the Dots* are from the Occupational Employment Survey. The wage estimates represent wages and salaries only and do not include nonproduction bonuses or employer costs of nonwage benefits such as health insurance or employer contributions to retirement plans. The information presented in *Connecting the Dots* includes median gross pay, exclusive of premium pay. The occupational median wage, or the 50th percentile, is the boundary between the highest paid 50 percent and the lowest paid 50 percent in the occupation. In other words, half the workers in the occupation earn more than the median wage, and half the workers earn less than the median wage.

Occupational Outlook Handbook: Much of the information regarding the training and education needed to enter and advance in careers, what workers do on the job, and the expected job prospects of careers in *Connecting the Dots* has been obtained from the Occupational Outlook Handbook.

 The following are the definitions for each type of postsecondary and work-related training used in *Connecting the Dots*. The descriptions reflect the United States Department of Labor, Bureau of Labor Statistics' definitions.

EDUCATION
Associate's degree: Degree completion typically requires at least 2 years of full-time academic study.

Bachelor's degree: Degree completion typically requires at least 4 years, but not more than 5 years, of full-time academic study.

Master's degree: Degree completion typically requires 1 or 2 years of full-time academic study beyond a bachelor's degree.

First professional degree: Degree completion typically requires at least 3 years of full-time academic study beyond a bachelor's degree.

Doctoral degree: Completion of a Ph.D. or other doctoral degree typically requires at least 3 years of full-time academic study beyond a bachelor's degree.

TRAINING

Short-term on-the-job training: Training is typically 1 month or less of on-the-job experience or instruction. Skills can be acquired during a short demonstration of job duties.

Moderate-term on-the-job training: Training includes 1 to 12 months of combined on-the-job experience and informal training.

Long-term on-the-job training: Training typically requires more than 12 months of on-the-job training or combined work experience and formal classroom instruction. Some include formal and informal apprenticeships that may last up to 5 years.

ACKNOWLEDGMENTS

Writing a book takes energy and determination, no doubt, but it also takes a lot of help—and truly, one of the biggest perks of writing a book for me is acknowledging and thanking all of those who were so integral in making this work come to be.

First, I acknowledge a place—my hometown. Kalamazoo, Michigan. In the fall of 2005, Kalamazoo became the setting for an innovative economic development experiment. That experiment is The Kalamazoo Promise, which is a scholarship program that pays up to 100 percent of tuition at any public college or university in Michigan for potentially all graduates of Kalamazoo Public Schools (KPS). Though a scholarship program, "The Promise" is considered a place-based economic development tool that has the potential to increase the human capital in the region and attract new businesses and families to Kalamazoo. Since the announcement of The Promise, educational, economic development, and civic community leaders have been collaborating to ensure that the greater Kalamazoo area leverages this scholarship program to increase economic vitality in the region.

Kalamazoo, Michigan, is also the home of the W.E. Upjohn Institute for Employment Research, which conducts research regarding the causes and effects of unemployment and measures for the alleviation of unemployment. It was my work at the Upjohn Institute that brought to light the need for a tool that connects the dots between education, interests, careers, and a successful life for students. That connect-the-dots tool became *Connecting the Dots Between Education, Interests, and Careers, Grades 7–10*. Working at the Upjohn Institute presented me with the opportunity to work with educational and workforce development experts from Kalamazoo Public Schools, The Kalamazoo Promise, and of course the Upjohn Institute.

I have received a great deal of support from my friends and colleagues in Kalamazoo who reviewed many drafts of the manuscript. In particular, my good friend Bridget Timmeney invested many hours working with me on *Connecting the Dots*. Bridget assisted with concept development, provided technical input, and offered editorial support. I am incredibly grateful for her assistance in this endeavor as well as for her friendship.

I also gratefully acknowledge Bob Jorth (Executive Administrator of the Kalamazoo Promise); Kevin Hollenbeck (Vice President and Senior Economist of the Upjohn Institute); Kate Cohler (Chicago Middle School Teacher); Michelle Miller-Adams (Visiting Scholar of the Upjohn Institute); Larry Trent; Ryan Carpenter, and Anne Kroemer for their editorial and technical support. Additionally, I am thankful to Randall Eberts (President of the Upjohn Institute) for encouraging me to continue working on *Connecting the Dots* after moving to Chicago to work at the Chicago Jobs Council, and Michael Rice, Ph.D. (Superintendent, Kalamazoo Public Schools), for supporting *Connecting the Dots*.

Many, many warm thanks also to the Tengelsen Family Foundation (TFF) for believing in me and in *Pass It On*, the earlier version of *Connecting the Dots*. TFF underwrote the publication of *Connecting the Dots*.

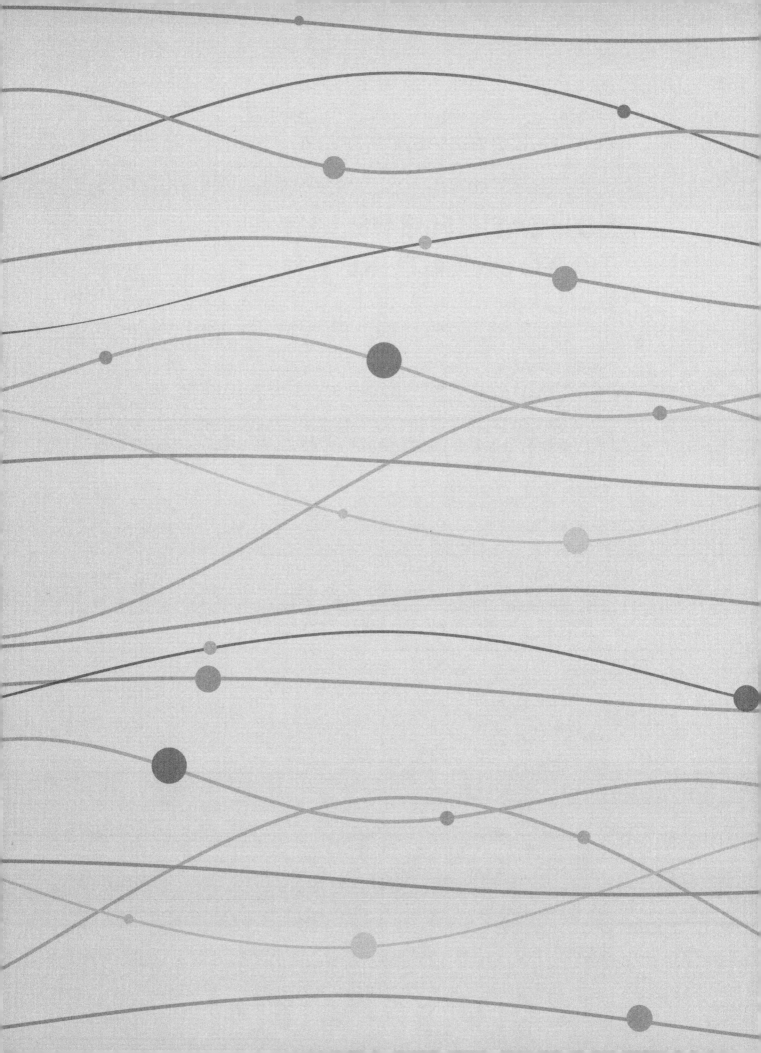

EDUCATION: THE KEY TO YOUR FUTURE

As adults we know that careers that pay more money generally require more education or training. "Education: The Key to Your Future" provides conversation starters for adults and helps them stress that students need to study now so that they can make money to pay their bills later. The section underscores that in order to get almost any job in the twenty-first century individuals will need at least a high school diploma. The topic addresses the fact that high school dropouts with a job make less money than individuals with a degree; high school dropouts make $454 per week, while high school graduates make $626 per week (median weekly earnings in 2009).[8] It helps teachers explain that the earnings continue to rise with educational attainment.

The section highlights the idea that people have to work to earn money to pay for the many costs associated with living. It provides discussion questions/answers for teachers to use to exemplify this. It identifies self-sufficiency and that individuals need to earn more than minimum wage and the poverty wage in order to be able to pay for the costs of living each month. It identifies that students will need a job when they get older because they will need to pay phone, grocery, car, rent or mortgage, garbage, and electricity bills.

The information helps students understand that they need to learn the material assigned by their teachers and do well in middle school, then high school and college or a training program, and then eventually find a career that they like. It also helps adults stress that the amount of money an individual earns isn't the only important thing to consider because happiness will depend on many factors: Family life, how much enjoyment is received in a career, and living a fulfilling life are just some factors.

 This icon identifies the material that can be downloaded and printed for students at **www.corwin.com/connectingthedots**.

1-1 THE COST OF LIVING

Matt is 18 years old and just graduated from high school in Illinois. He is moving out of his parents' house to live on his own. His parents told him that he will need to learn to budget his money because each month he will need to pay his bills on time. How much money do you think it will cost Matt to live alone each month?

 A $ 500 ✔ **B** $1,800 **C** $4,000

Summary: In order to be self-sufficient* it will cost Matt at least $1,800 to live each month, and over the course of the year it will cost him $21,250.[9] In order to make $1,800 a month Matt will need to earn a wage of $10.06 an hour, which is more than Illinois' minimum wage ($8.00/hour) and its poverty wage ($8.67 per hour).[10] And still, it will actually be hard to live on $1,800 a month. This amount only covers the necessities: food, housing, transportation (e.g., car, insurance, gas and maintenance), health care, clothing, phone, personal items, and taxes. Explain that taxes are taken out of a paycheck to pay for local, state, and federal services (police and fire departments, post office, and other things). If Matt wants to go on trips, to the movies, or out to dinner or pursue other fun things, he will have to make more money than $1,800 per month.

Explain that to live a comfortable life students will need to be able to pay for all of these necessities and fun things; to do this, they will need a good job. Usually, the more education or training they get, the more money they can make in a job, which will help them pay bills and enjoy life.

* Self-sufficiency is what it costs to make ends meet without public or private assistance.

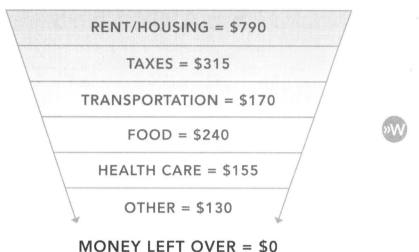

COST OF LIVING FOR ONE MONTH
$1,800 PER MONTH

RENT/HOUSING = $790
TAXES = $315
TRANSPORTATION = $170
FOOD = $240
HEALTH CARE = $155
OTHER = $130

MONEY LEFT OVER = $0

Lead the students in a discussion of how much money it costs to live for one month. Show them the list of average monthly costs that a single adult living in Illinois needs to budget. The information above describes what is necessary to budget for an adult living alone in Illinois.[11] Remind students that $1,800 per month can be spent very quickly when it costs more than $200 a month to buy groceries and usually more than $700 dollars a month for housing.

To highlight how quickly money can be spent, ask students to determine how much money it would cost them to eat at their favorite fast-food chain every day on their lunch break, Monday through Friday (five times a week), for four weeks. If the meal they like costs $5.00, then they will have to pay $5.00, five days a week. The cost per week would be $5.00 per meal x 5 days a week = $25 per week, and the cost per month would be $25.00 per week x 4 weeks = $100. The student, according to this example, would have used $100 on 25 meals of the $240 dollars that is budgeted for food. The student has only $140 dollars left, and if eating three meals a day, the student has 59 more meals that have to be paid for (3 meals x 7 days per week = 21 meals per week, and 21 meals per week x 4 weeks a month = 84 meals, so 84 meals – 25 meals = 59 meals left over for the rest of the month). This leaves only $2.37 per meal ($140 left in the budget/59 meals) for each meal for the rest of the month.

1-2 DROPOUTS EARN LESS

Jessie and Kevin are both 17 years old and would have been in their senior year of high school together. However, Jessie dropped out of school. Kevin decided to stay in high school and is graduating and receiving his high school diploma. Jessie has been looking for a job because she lives on her own and needs to pay her bills. She is learning the hard way that without a high school diploma, she may not be able to get a job that pays enough money to pay her bills. On average, how much money do you think a high school dropout with a job makes per week?

Ⓐ $ 100   ✔Ⓑ $454   Ⓒ $850

Summary: Jessie has found out that it is really hard to get a job without a high school diploma. For the jobs she qualifies for, she can make an average of only about $454 per week,[12] or about $1,800 per month ($450 × 4 weeks = $1,800 per month simple estimate). This might sound like a lot of money, but when you consider the costs of living you get a different picture. Jessie will have to budget for rent/housing, transportation, food, health care, taxes, and other necessities. Clearly, the $454 per week is not a lot of money in light of all of the budget considerations. What if she wants to do something else with her money? What if she wants to see a movie or buy new clothes? If she wants to use some of her money for entertainment, her monthly bills will add up. How will she earn extra money?

* The data represent annual averages for individuals age 25 and over. Data represent earnings before taxes and other deductions and include any overtime pay, commissions, or tips usually received.

Jessie's friend Kevin, who earned his high school diploma, can make an average of $170 more a week than Jessie. Comparing Jessie and Kevin over the course of a month, Kevin will make $700 more per month, which will make paying his bills much easier and provide him with extra money to use for entertainment or to save. Making money isn't the only important thing in life, but it is important that you have enough to pay for your basic needs. Life really is more fun if you can pay for entertainment, too.

EDUCATION & INCOME: INCOME OVER ONE YEAR

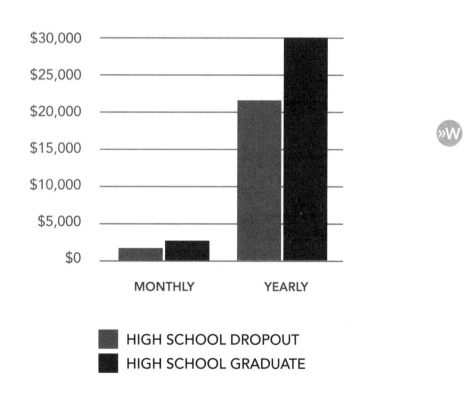

■ HIGH SCHOOL DROPOUT
■ HIGH SCHOOL GRADUATE

Source: Bureau of Labor Statistics, Current Population Survey. The data for the monthly and yearly categories in the chart are projected from the weekly earnings information obtained from the Current Population Survey. To determine monthly and yearly projections, each educational level was multiplied by 4 (weeks) and 12 (months), respectively. These are simple estimations.

1-3 COLLEGE GRADS EARN MORE

Kerwin's mom nags him all the time that he'd better stay in school, get his high school diploma, and then go to college or get a training certificate. She tells him that if he doesn't graduate from college or at least high school he is more likely to be unemployed and it will be harder to pay his bills. His mom recently told him that college graduates make $400 more a week than high school graduates and $570 more than high school dropouts. Do you think what his mom said is true or false?

 **A** True   **B** False

Summary: Kerwin's mom was right. If Kerwin earns his college degree, he will likely make $400 more a week than a high school graduate and $570 more than a high school dropout.[13] He will make $2,300 more a month than a high school dropout and more than $27,000 more in one year. Kerwin will make more than $19,000 more each year than someone with a high school diploma. The General Rule: The more education a person has, the more likely that person will get a job and the more that person will earn in his or her lifetime. If Kerwin gets more education or training after high school, Kerwin will be able to make more money and more easily pay his bills and pay for things to enjoy life (such as entertainment) when he grows up.

INCOME DIFFERENCES BY EDUCATIONAL ATTAINMENT

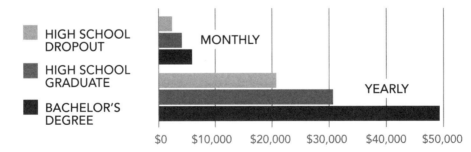

Source: Bureau of Labor Statistics, Current Population Survey. The data for the monthly and yearly categories in the chart are projected from the weekly earnings information obtained from the Current Population Survey. To determine monthly and yearly projections, weekly earnings for each educational level were multiplied by 4 (weeks) and 12 (months), respectively. These are simple estimations.

1-4 COLLEGE: NOT THE ONLY ROUTE TO SUCCESS

Dusty really wants to be an electrician and is thinking about going to a community college to do an apprenticeship—a combination of on-the-job training and classroom work. Dusty was talking with some of his friends who are planning to go to college to get their bachelor's degrees. His friends told him that people who do apprenticeship programs will make less money than people who go to college. True or false?

Summary: What Dusty's friends told him is false. Dusty needs to know that, in many cases, apprenticeships and on-the-job training can help people earn as much money as people who earn bachelor's degrees. The type of education or training you will need depends on what you want to do when you grow up. You should also spend some time thinking about your skills and interests. Dusty knows that he wants to be an electrician; he likes the idea of working with electricity and wires and fixing electrical problems in homes and businesses. He's learned that he can do that through an apprenticeship program. Other career areas you can pursue through apprenticeships include health care, construction, manufacturing, and technology.*

 The table on the next page lists careers with apprenticeships.

* Some jobs with above-average earnings do not require a bachelor's degree, but most require substantial training.

CAREER*	EDUCATION*	INCOME**
CARPENTERS They build, install, and repair things that are usually made of wood.	3–4 YEARS	$39,470
CHEFS, HEAD COOKS They oversee food service of a restaurant.	2 YEARS	$40,090
DENTAL ASSISTANTS They provide patient care, office, and laboratory duties. Activities might include disinfecting equipment, preparing tools used to treat patients, and updating records.	1–2 YEARS	$33,230
ELEVATOR INSTALLERS/REPAIRERS They put together, install, and replace elevators, escalators, moving walkways, etc.	4 YEARS	$69,050
EMERGENCY MEDICAL TECHNICIANS They assess injuries, administer emergency medical care, and transport the sick or injured to medical facilities.	1–2 YEARS	$30,000
HEATING, AIR CONDITIONING, REFRIGERATION MECHANICS They install or repair heating, air conditioning, or refrigeration systems.	6 MONTHS TO 2 YEARS	$41,100

JEWELERS They design, make, fix, and determine the cost of metals and gems.	1 YEAR OR MORE	$34,060
PLUMBERS They put together, install, and repair pipelines that carry water, steam, air, or other liquids.	4–5 YEARS	$46,320
SHEET METAL WORKERS They make, put together, install, and repair sheet metal products.	4–5 YEARS	$40,640

* Bureau of Labor Statistics, U.S. Department of Labor. Occupational Handbook, 2010–11 Edition.
** Bureau of Labor Statistics, U.S. Department of Labor, Occupational Employment Statistics.

1-5 SUPPORTING A FAMILY IS EXPENSIVE

Theresa is a ninth grader and has five brothers and sisters. She knows that when she grows up she wants to have at least four children. She told her dad this, and he said, "It's expensive to raise kids, and the more kids you have, the more money you need to feed them and pay the monthly bills." His advice to her was that she needs to study hard and graduate from high school and go to college so she can make enough money to support her family. He said that, usually, the more education people get beyond high school, the more money they will earn in their jobs. Do you think the advice Theresa's dad gave her is true or false?

 ✔Ⓐ True   Ⓑ False

Summary: The advice Theresa's dad gave Theresa is true. Earning an associate's degree, a specialized-skills-training certificate or a bachelor's degree can increase your earnings and give you the skills you will need in the workforce. If Theresa wants a big family, she must be sure that she can get a job where she will make enough money to raise her kids and pay her monthly bills. For example, the self-sufficiency wage in the state of Illinois for a single person is $10.06 an hour, but for a family with two adults, a preschooler, an elementary school student, and a teenager, both adults have to earn $14.25 an hour. To highlight this, the single person has to make $21,247 a year just to make ends meet, and the family in the example has to earn $60,188 to make ends meet.[14] If Theresa wants a large family she is going to have to find a job where she can earn enough money to support the family. Theresa's dad also could have told her that in the future about two out of three jobs will require at least some college education. Remember that the more your job matches your skills and interests, the happier you will be working at that job every day. And the more education you have, the more employers will consider hiring you.

SUPPLEMENTAL DISCUSSION

Why Some People Make More Money

Ask the students to identify two reasons some people make more money than other people.

Suggested talking points for facilitators:

A. It's usually the case that the higher the level of education you earn, the more money you will earn.

B. The longer you've worked in your job, the more money you will make.

C. The career you choose will have an effect on how much money you make.

MORE EDUCATION = BETTER-PAYING JOBS

"More Education = Better-Paying Jobs" emphasizes that to get almost any job in the twenty-first century economy, individuals need at least a high school diploma. This is important to highlight for students because by 2018, sixty-three percent[15] of job openings will require workers to have at least some college education, which means that individuals will need at least a high school education and education beyond high school. Currently, in the United States, only about 70 percent of students graduate from public high schools with a diploma (the graduation rate varies based on the method of calculation).[16] This section provides adults with discussion topics that will help students understand why they should graduate from high school. This section also emphasizes the importance of college, apprenticeship, and other types of training programs. Different options for postsecondary training are presented because college represents only 35 percent of the United States' postsecondary education and training system.[17]

This section helps adults direct students to identify their interests—and emphasizes that jobs based on their interests will likely require education beyond high school. It highlights that individuals with more education or skill-specific training are more likely to advance in their careers.

SUBJECTS COVERED IN THIS TOPIC

 This icon identifies the material that can be downloaded and printed for students at **www.corwin.com/connectingthedots.**

2-1 HOW MANY STUDENTS GRADUATE?

Lillian's dad tells her repeatedly that it is really important that she finish high school and learn all the things her teacher asks her to learn so that when she gets into the "real world" she can get a job. Lillian's dad really likes numbers and gives her interesting facts to consider. He asks her, "What is the graduation rate for public schools in the United States?" What do you think is the right answer?

  A 70%   **B** 80%   **C** 92%

Summary: The correct answer is 70 percent.[18] If you look around you and pick ten students (or think of ten students), this means that on average three of the ten people in that group will not get their high school diplomas. Most jobs in the United States require people to have at least a high school diploma. People who don't graduate from high school have a harder time getting jobs than people with their diplomas or higher education.

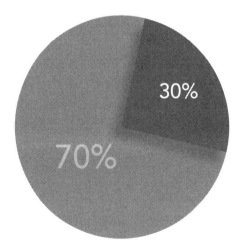

Who Will Be Left Out?

Have students work in small groups. Tell students to make a list of at least three events that draw a large crowd (such as a specific concert or sporting event). Have students gather facts (using the Internet) about the average attendance at each event. Tell students to research and identify photos representing the crowd at each type of event. Have students highlight or color a portion of each image to represent 30 percent. As a class, have students share their examples, photos, and facts. Discuss what it means for that portion of the population to have not graduated from high school. Ask: What are the consequences of not graduating from high school?

2-2 WE WANT YOU TO SUCCEED

Trina's teacher tells Trina and her classmates that they should finish high school and earn college degrees or get on-the-job training so that they get jobs they like when they are older. Trina gets sick of everybody telling her what to do and of grown-ups thinking they know everything. Her teacher really just wants the best for Trina and her classmates and for the class to have great lives, to have jobs they like, and to be able to pay their bills. Trina is likely to get a good job if she does which of the following? (There is more than one correct answer.)

(A) Does not earn a high school diploma

(B) Earns only a high school diploma

✔**(C)** Earns an associate's degree

✔**(D)** Gets on-the-job or short-term training

✔**(E)** Earns a bachelor's degree

Summary: Trina is likely to get a job that she likes and will help her pay her bills if she earns an associate's degree, gets on-the-job or short-term training, or gets a bachelor's degree or more. In fact, some education after high school will be needed for many of the jobs that will be available when you graduate from high school. And on-the-job training is the most important for 12 of the 20 largest-growing jobs.[19] (See page 41 for "Twenty Fastest-Growing Jobs.") It is important to consider what you like to do when deciding what to do after high school. In some cases, specialized training will be needed for you to get the job you want, while in other cases you will need to get a college degree. The decisions you make now about your own studying and education will make a difference to your own quality of life in the future.

 The table on the next page lists the careers with the largest growth over the 2008–2018 period.

STATS OF NOTE

CAREER*	EDUCATION*	INCOME**
HOME HEALTH AIDES They provide personal health care to patients, such as bathing, dressing, and grooming individuals at home or a care facility.	SHORT-TERM ON-THE-JOB TRAINING	$20,480
CUSTOMER SERVICE REPRESENTATIVES They interact with customers and provide them with responses to questions about products and services.	SHORT-TERM ON-THE-JOB TRAINING	$30,290
COMBINED FOOD PREPARATION AND SERVING WORKERS, INCLUDING FAST FOOD They perform duties that combine food preparation and food service.	SHORT-TERM ON-THE-JOB TRAINING	$17,220
PERSONAL AND HOME CARE AIDES They help elderly or disabled adults with daily living activities (making beds, doing laundry, cooking) at the patient's home or in a daytime facility.	SHORT-TERM ON-THE-JOB TRAINING	$19,680
RETAIL SALESPEOPLE They sell items, such as furniture, vehicles, appliances, and clothing.	SHORT-TERM ON-THE-JOB TRAINING	$20,260
OFFICE CLERKS, GENERAL They carry out duties such as answering phones, bookkeeping, typing, office machine operation, and filing.	SHORT-TERM ON-THE-JOB TRAINING	$34,060

CONSTRUCTION LABORERS They perform tasks that require physical labor like building highways, carrying out construction projects, and demolishing sites.	MODERATE-TERM ON-THE-JOB TRAINING	$29,150
TRUCK DRIVERS, HEAVY AND TRACTOR-TRAILER They drive a tractor-trailer or a truck to transport and deliver goods, livestock, and other materials. They may be required to unload the truck.	SHORT-TERM ON-THE-JOB TRAINING	$37,730
LANDSCAPING AND GROUNDSKEEPING WORKERS They landscape or maintain grounds of property using hand or power tools. They do things like lay sod, mow, plant, water, and install sprinklers.	SHORT-TERM ON-THE-JOB TRAINING	$23,480
BOOKKEEPERS, ACCOUNTANTS, AND AUDITORS They compute and record and check data for accuracy to keep financial records.	MODERATE-TERM ON-THE-JOB TRAINING	$33,450
RECEPTIONISTS AND INFORMATION CLERKS They answer questions and obtain information for customers and visitors. They provide information about activities conducted at the office or location.	SHORT-TERM ON-THE-JOB TRAINING	$25,070

* *Bureau of Labor Statistics, U.S. Department of Labor: Occupational Handbook, 2010–11 Edition.*
** *Bureau of Labor Statistics, U.S. Department of Labor, Occupational Employment Statistics.*

MORE EDUCATION = BETTER-PAYING JOBS

2-3 DROPOUTS OFTEN DON'T GET JOBS

You have probably heard that if you don't graduate from high school, you are going to have a really hard time getting a job. In 2008, what percentage of people 25 years old and older who didn't graduate from high school participated in the labor force?*

  A 92%   ✔**B** 64%   **C** 44%

Summary: In 2008, only 64 percent of people aged 25 and older who didn't complete high school participated in the labor force.[20] This means that 36 percent did not. For 16- to 19-year-olds, only 31 percent of students who weren't enrolled in school participated in the labor force. How does this population pay their bills? The good thing is that 86 percent of people 25 years old and over with at least a bachelor's degree had jobs.[21] This shows that people with higher levels of education are more likely to have jobs. Getting a job may seem really far off, but time flies, and soon you will need a job so that you can pay your own bills. Not only are you more likely to have a job with higher levels of education, but the amount of money you can earn generally increases with education. Earnings also increase with experience. This means it will be easier for you to pay your bills and also have an opportunity to buy goods and services (clothes, movies, etc.) that you enjoy.

* Labor force participation rate is the percentage of the population who are employed or seeking employment.

No Jobs for Some Who Drop Out

Ask students to imagine a group of 20 people who are 16 to 19 years old and have all dropped out of high school. Next, tell students that 14 of these students represent the students who dropped out of high school and did not participate in the labor force. Let them know that the six students (or 30 percent) left represent the number of students who did not graduate from high school and were fortunate to get jobs.

A. Ask the students to discuss, or write, what it would mean to be among the 20 dropouts in terms of getting a job and paying bills.

B. Then ask them to talk, or write, about how their life might be different if they were among the six who got jobs but still didn't graduate from high school. (Even though these students found jobs, they will still have a hard time paying their bills because jobs that require less than a high school diploma are extremely low paying. Additionally, these jobs will not be career-track jobs, meaning students will have a very hard time advancing within their company.)

C. If you have time, ask the students to discuss, or write about, how their life might differ if they decided to stay in school and graduate from high school or get their bachelor's degree. (Note that 76 percent of individuals 25 and older who graduated from high school and 86 percent who had their bachelor's degree or higher were employed in 2008.[22])

2-4 TWO-YEAR PROGRAMS CAN BE A GOOD OPTION

Jackson isn't sure whether he should go to a two-year community college, a technical school, or a four-year college and get a bachelor's degree after high school. He's heard that going to a community college or technical training school is not a good idea and that he should get his bachelor's degree if he wants to get a job when he is done with school. Is what he heard true or false?

 Ⓐ True ✔Ⓑ False

Summary: False. The type of training Jackson should get depends on what he wants to do. Community colleges can provide the skills you need to be successful in many fields. Going to a community college is also less expensive than a four-year school, so you can save money by going to a community college. Some people start at a community college and then transfer to a four-year college to finish the remaining two years. Community colleges can help students develop study habits for four-year colleges and universities. You can earn an associate's degree from a community college to be a dental assistant or computer-support specialist. A typical dental assistant can earn $33,230 a year, and a typical computer support specialist can earn $44,300 (median).[23,24]

2-5 THE ADVANTAGE OF AN ADVANCED DEGREE

Johnny is in eighth grade, earns all A's, and works really hard in school. One reason he works hard is that he knows that if he wants to get a good job—a job that he enjoys and that will pay enough money to cover his bills—he will have to go to college. Johnny was listening to the news with his mom, and the news broadcaster said that people with master's degrees are more likely to have jobs than people with bachelor's degrees. There may be several reasons this is true. Of the following, which one do you think is one of those reasons?

✓**A** A master's degree is more specialized than a bachelor's degree.

B A master's degree is less specialized than a bachelor's degree.

C A bachelor's degree is easy to earn.

Summary: In 2009, the unemployment rate* of people with master's degrees who didn't have a job was 3.9 percent; for people with bachelor's degrees the rate was 5.2 percent.[25] People with master's degrees are more likely to have jobs than people with bachelor's degrees because, in part, a master's degree is more specialized than a bachelor's degree. People who earn master's degrees also are usually a little older, more mature, and have some work experience in their fields. By earning an advanced degree, they have demonstrated a willingness to work hard.

* Individuals are considered unemployed if they do not have a job, have looked for a job in the prior four weeks, and are available for work.

SUPPLEMENTAL DISCUSSION

Why Go to College?

Tell students that almost all employers require their employees to have high school diplomas. Ask students to discuss how that relates to them. Consider moving the conversation along by talking about the fact that a job provides money that will pay for groceries, rent, cars, phone, and clothes. Point out that a high school diploma is just a step in the education ladder that they need to get into a college or a training program. For postsecondary education, or school after high school, it is important to decide what you want to be, or at least what your career interests are, because this will help you decide what degree you need. Sometimes a certificate will be good enough; other times an associate's degree is all you need; but sometimes the career you are interested in will require at least a bachelor's degree.[26]

 The table on the next page lists the twenty fastest-growing jobs, which require a range of education and training (on-the-job training to bachelor's, master's, and doctoral degrees).

STATS OF NOTE

CAREER*	EDUCATION*	INCOME**
BIOMEDICAL ENGINEERS They apply knowledge of engineering, biology, and biomechanical principles to the design, development, and evaluation of biological and health systems and products.	BACHELOR'S DEGREE	$78,860
NETWORK SYSTEMS AND DATA COMMUNICATIONS ANALYSTS They analyze, design, test, and evaluate network systems, such as local area networks (LAN), wide area networks (WAN), Internet, and intranet.	BACHELOR'S DEGREE	$73,250
HOME HEALTH AIDES They provide routine personal health care, such as bathing, dressing, or grooming, to elderly, convalescent, or disabled persons in the home of patients or in a residential care facility.	SHORT-TERM ON-THE-JOB TRAINING	$20,480
PERSONAL AND HOME CARE AIDES They assist elderly or disabled adults with daily living activities at the person's home or in a daytime nonresidential facility.	SHORT-TERM ON-THE-JOB TRAINING	$19,680
FINANCIAL EXAMINERS They enforce or ensure compliance with laws and regulations governing financial and securities institutions and financial and real estate transactions.	BACHELOR'S DEGREE	$71,750

STATS OF NOTE

CAREER*	EDUCATION*	INCOME**
MEDICAL SCIENTISTS, EXCEPT EPIDEMIOLOGISTS They conduct research dealing with the understanding of human diseases and the improvement of human health.	DOCTORAL DEGREE	$74,590
PHYSICIAN ASSISTANTS They provide health care services typically performed by a physician, under the supervision of a physician.	MASTER'S DEGREE	$84,420
SKIN CARE SPECIALISTS They provide skin care treatments to face and body to enhance an individual's appearance.	POSTSECONDARY VOCATIONAL AWARD	$28,580
BIOCHEMISTS AND BIOPHYSICISTS They study the chemical composition and physical principles of living cells and organisms, their electrical and mechanical energy, and related phenomena.	DOCTORAL DEGREE	$82,390
ATHLETIC TRAINERS They evaluate, advise, and treat athletes to assist in recovery from injury, avoiding injury, or maintaining peak physical fitness.	BACHELOR'S DEGREE	$41,340
PHYSICAL THERAPIST AIDES They work with a physical therapist or physical therapy assistant, to perform tasks in specific situations.	SHORT-TERM ON-THE-JOB TRAINING	$23,890

Occupation	Education/Training	Median Salary
DENTAL HYGIENISTS They clean teeth and examine oral areas, head, and neck for signs of oral disease.	ASSOCIATE'S DEGREE	$66,340
VETERINARY TECHNOLOGISTS AND TECHNICIANS They perform medical tests in a laboratory environment for use in the treatment and diagnosis of diseases in animals.	ASSOCIATE'S DEGREE	$29,280
DENTAL ASSISTANTS They assist dentists, set up patients and equipment, and keep records.	MODERATE-TERM ON-THE-JOB TRAINING	$33,230
COMPUTER SOFTWARE ENGINEERS, APPLICATIONS They develop, create, and modify general computer applications software or specialized utility programs.	BACHELOR'S DEGREE	$87,480
MEDICAL ASSISTANTS They perform administrative and certain clinical duties under the direction of physician.	MODERATE-TERM ON-THE-JOB TRAINING	$28,650
PHYSICAL THERAPIST ASSISTANTS They assist physical therapists in providing physical therapy treatments and procedures.	ASSOCIATE'S DEGREE	$48,290

CAREER*	EDUCATION*	INCOME**
VETERINARIANS They diagnose and treat diseases and dysfunctions of animals.	FIRST PROFESSIONAL DEGREE	$80,510
SELF-ENRICHMENT EDUCATION TEACHERS They teach or instruct courses other than those that normally lead to an occupational objective or degree.	WORK EXPERIENCE IN A RELATED OCCUPATION	$36,440
COMPLIANCE OFFICERS, EXCEPT AGRICULTURE, CONSTRUCTION, HEALTH AND SAFETY, AND TRANSPORTATION They evaluate and investigate eligibility and conformity with laws and regulations.	LONG-TERM ON-THE-JOB TRAINING	$47,050

* Bureau of Labor Statistics, U.S. Department of Labor. Occupational Handbook, 2010–11 Edition.
** Bureau of Labor Statistics, U.S. Department of Labor, Occupational Employment Statistics.

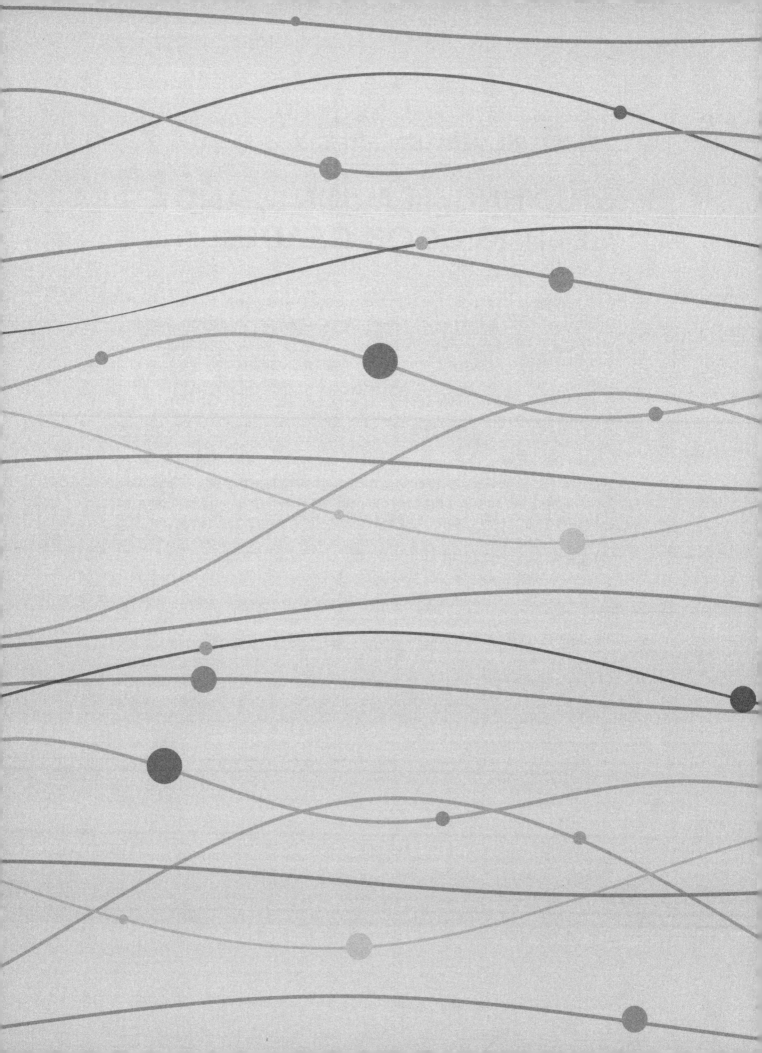

STUDYING, LEARNING, AND GETTING GOOD GRADES

"Studying, Learning, and Getting Good Grades" highlights the importance of doing well in terms of grades and academics. This section provides students with insights about the connection between studying and learning. It includes conversation starters regarding getting good grades and what it means to get good grades and provides methods for doing so in an interesting and didactic format. It reminds students that studying is a skill and emphasizes that to become good at it they must practice just as they would for their sport or hobby. It gives examples of good study habits like note taking (i.e., record, reduce, recite, reflect, review), being well organized, and finding a safe, comfortable place to study. It highlights for students why they need to be able to read and write outside the classroom, in the real world.

Keeping students engaged in school is often difficult. A facilitated discussion about why studying is important provides students with a way to connect the dots between good study skills and career success. This section highlights how the development of study skills in middle school will help make the transition to high school easier. Students enjoy having discussions in school that have no clear answers, and this section includes questions that provoke intrigue and engagement. It reminds students that achieving good grades is not the only goal of studying and that they should be mindful of taking challenging courses so that they learn more.

SUBJECTS COVERED IN THIS TOPIC

3-1 How to Get Good Grades

3-2 Reading Is the Foundation

3-3 Making the Most of Study Time

3-4 Think Beyond Getting Good Grades

3-5 Challenge Yourself

 This icon identifies the material that can be downloaded and printed for students at **www.corwin.com/connectingthedots.**

3-1 HOW TO GET GOOD GRADES

Although you may not believe it, your teachers don't want to torture you by making you do homework. They want you to learn the material they give you so that you can do well in middle school, and in high school, and eventually find a career that you like. Describe three strategies you can use to help you improve your academic performance.

SUGGESTED ANSWERS

A Do all your homework. If you don't understand something, ask your teacher or a classmate for help so that you can learn the material.

B Be well organized.

C Find a place to study where you can concentrate and learn.

D Have all your study materials at your study spot.

E Take notes on what the teacher says.

F Sit in the front of the class.

Summary: You should be organized, manage your study time, and complete your homework. Taking notes on the main points that your teacher makes is another strategy; it is a skill that you will get better at over time. Think about work first, play later. Doing your homework in front of the TV is a bad idea because you are less likely to give all your attention to your homework. The information is less likely to sink in, and you're less likely to remember it when you need it later. Sitting in the front of the class instead of the back also usually helps students improve their academic performance.

Note to Self

Ask students to describe their best note-taking strategies. Have them work with a partner and discuss their own strategies for taking notes. Ask: What is difficult or challenging about taking notes? What strategies work for you? Have students write at least three ways they will improve this skill as part of their studying routine. Talking points might include explaining that note taking is a skill that needs to be practiced in order to be good at it. Tell students that even college students sometimes think that taking notes is challenging. Five tips you can provide to students come from the Cornell Note-Taking System:

1. Record. During the lecture, record as many important facts as possible.

2. Reduce. As soon after class as possible, summarize the main ideas and facts. Summarizing reinforces learning and helps students remember important factual relationships.

3. Recite. This helps students remember the summarized facts in their long-term memory.

4. Reflect. The notes are in the student's own words, and reflecting trains the mind to categorize important information, which leads to better memorization.

5. Review. The students should review the notes quickly and regularly. The notes have been summarized, which helps the students remember a lot of information.

The Cornell Note-Taking System is a great resource for teaching students how to take notes. It is a highly recommended resource according to middle school teachers in the Chicago Public Schools. http://coe.jmu.edu/learningtoolbox/cornellnotes.html.

3-2 READING IS THE FOUNDATION

Other than to get good grades, why do you need to be able to read well? Describe at least four reasons.

SUGGESTED ANSWERS

Ⓐ To get information online.

Ⓑ To read road signs to drive a car.

Ⓒ To think critically about what you read.

Ⓓ To play video games.

Ⓔ To read books and comic books for fun.

Summary: Knowing how to read can help you get good grades and help you prepare for college, but you also need to read beyond doing your homework. In most jobs that you will have, you will not only need to know how to read, but you will also need to be able to think critically about what you read. Thinking critically includes thinking about what you're reading, understanding the content, and asking yourself if the content makes sense. No matter what you want to be when you grow up, you will need to read every day. You need to read and write when you interact online, when you are at work, and when you are enjoying fun activities like playing video games and shopping. In fact, you need to read critically to understand information when you go shopping.

You can practice reading and writing skills by e-mailing, working online, reading the sports section of the newspaper or magazines, or reading books or comic books that you like.

3-3 MAKING THE MOST OF STUDY TIME

Terence gets A's and B's in high school. When asked how he does it, he says that in middle school he struggled to get good grades and that one of his teachers gave him some strategies that help him focus and study. He uses those same strategies in high school. Describe three strategies that he might use.

SUGGESTED ANSWERS

A Planning daily times to study.

B Learning how to take notes in class that help with studying at home.

C Turn off the TV set.

D Gathering the necessary materials at the place where you study.

Summary: Planning daily study times, taking notes, finding a quiet study spot, and making sure that you have all the necessary materials to study are all good study habits.[27] Think twice about doing homework with friends because you may waste too much time socializing. If you like studying with others, try to choose one study buddy whom you can work with and learn with. An important study skill to develop is taking notes. It is an important skill because you can use the notes you take in class to study for tests. At first taking notes can be hard, but if you practice you will develop this skill, and you will be able to use your notes to study for tests, making test taking easier. Remember that you don't have to take notes on everything the teacher says. Focusing only on the important parts of what a teacher says is a way to focus your studying. If you need help developing these skills or think you are falling behind your classmates, ask your teacher or counselor for help.

A Tale of Two Students

Ask students to write stories about two fictional classmates: Lance, who has good study habits, and T.R., who has bad study habits. Students should describe Lance's and T.R.'s study habits and the consequences of their study habits, and explain why they are good or poor habits. To help students get started, ask: What are three good study habits? What are three poor habits that prevent someone from getting homework done? What do good study habits "look" like?

3-4 THINK BEYOND GETTING GOOD GRADES

Getting good grades in high school automatically means you will do well in college or a career. True or false?

A True ✔**B** False

Summary: False. Getting good grades will help you get into college and may help you get a good job, but getting good grades doesn't guarantee success. Earning good grades is just one thing that will help you get ready for life after high school. You should study to learn and be curious and, as a result, get good grades. High academic performance means you learned and mastered the material; this effort or ability often reflects a work ethic that is attractive to college admissions officers and employers. Many students may be nervous about doing well in college; you're not alone if you worry about this. In high school, don't just study, but practice and learn how to study. Along the way, you're also developing problem-solving skills and learning to make connections and think critically. Most good students have strategies for studying to develop these skills. Once you learn to study, chances are you'll do fine. If you still need help, teachers are good resources, and so are tutors.

3-5 CHALLENGE YOURSELF

If Maria takes easier classes than Brandon and they both get B's, then Brandon will most likely be chosen over Maria by a college. True or false?

 **A** True   **B** False

Summary: True. Brandon would most likely be chosen over Maria by a college. Colleges think that someone who takes harder classes is more motivated and willing to work hard than someone who takes easier classes. High academic performance does not necessarily mean just getting good grades; it is also important to take difficult classes and challenge yourself to show colleges that you have a good education and are a hard worker. Since learning is lifelong, it's helpful to show you are willing to learn.

SUPPLEMENTAL DISCUSSION

Define Your Goals

Ask students to write two lists: 1) five educational goals that they want to accomplish by the time they are 25 years old; and 2) five career goals that they want to accomplish by the time they are 25 years old. (Examples of goals are graduating from high school, an apprenticeship or training program, college; attaining a specific job; earning a certain salary.) Ask them to identify why each goal is a priority, what accomplishing the goals will afford them, and how they plan to reach each goal.

SCHOOL SUBJECTS AND HOW THEY RELATE TO CAREERS

"School Subjects and How They Relate to Careers" answers the "why" questions. When your students ask "why do I need to learn this?" you can answer by explaining the value of math, reading, social studies, science, and language arts classes. Students have a hard time understanding (and sometimes have difficulty believing) that the classes that they take are building blocks for their future education, career, and life. The ability for people to match education with career alternatives is very important, yet this is largely an underdeveloped skill set for students in the United States.[28] Helping students understand the relationship between education and careers will enable them to understand the impact that education will have on their lives and help keep them engaged in school in the short term, and in the long run help students make informed educational and career decisions. Having conversations that connect education and training is increasingly important for people of all ages because this knowledge is key to obtaining employment.[29]

This section provides examples of why subjects taken in school are important. It helps students to make the connection between classes they take now and how they will use the skills developed in those classes in specific careers. The section provides descriptions of all of the careers that are featured in this section so that students are aware of the wide variety of jobs available in the labor market. This will also help students start thinking about and discussing what they might like to do when they grow up.

SUBJECTS COVERED IN THIS TOPIC

4-1 Math Skills Are Important

4-2 Reading and Writing, They're Vital

4-3 How Society Works

4-4 Science Teaches Critical Thinking

4-5 Language Insights

 This icon identifies the material that can be downloaded and printed for students at **www.corwin.com/connectingthedots.**

4-1 MATH SKILLS ARE IMPORTANT

Sydney is a seventh grader and has a hard time believing that having math skills is important for her future. She doesn't think she will need math and argues with her math teacher that math is unnecessary. Sydney's teacher tells her that not only will she need to use math every day when she grows up, but that she uses it every day in school. Do you think what her teacher said is true or false?

 ✓Ⓐ True   Ⓑ False

Summary: Sydney's teacher was right. People of all ages and at all stages of their careers use math. Learning math prepares you for life regardless of what you do for a job. Math skills help you solve more problems than you may realize. You need math skills for almost every job you can think of. In the health care field, doctors and nurses apply math skills to measure and weigh patients and evaluate test results. In the hospitality field (retail, restaurants, and hotels), cashiers need to make change for customers. People in the construction field need math skills to measure quantities and dimensions for building. You also need math to work in engineering, technology, and business. Whether it's multiplication, geometry, or algebra, you need math to make all kinds of daily decisions.

»Ⓦ The table on the next page lists careers that require strong math skills.

CAREER*	EDUCATION*	INCOME**
ACTUARIES They use math, statistics, and financial theory to consider the risk that an event will happen and help businesses develop policies that minimize the cost of that risk.	BACHELOR'S DEGREE AND LONG-TERM ON-THE-JOB TRAINING	$87,650
ARCHITECTS They draw and design homes, buildings, parks, and other structures. They are trained to develop the idea of what a structure will look like and turn the idea into images for clients to look at and builders to use to build the structure.	BACHELOR'S DEGREE AND INTERNSHIP/ RESIDENCY	$72,550
OPERATIONS RESEARCH ANALYSTS They help organizations solve problems and make better decisions.	BACHELOR'S DEGREE	$70,960
FINANCIAL ANALYSTS They help individuals, families, and businesses make decisions about how to save and invest their money.	BACHELOR'S DEGREE	$74,350
STATISTICIANS They use math to analyze and interpret data and draw conclusions.	MASTER'S DEGREE	$72,830
ECONOMISTS They collect and consider data and look for trends in the economy. They also research how society distributes land, work, social services, and machinery to produce goods and services.	BACHELOR'S DEGREE, MASTER'S DEGREE	$86,930

* Bureau of Labor Statistics, U.S. Department of Labor: Occupational Handbook, 2010–11 Edition.
** Bureau of Labor Statistics, U.S. Department of Labor, Occupational Employment Statistics.

Math, Math Everywhere

Ask students to brainstorm and describe daily tasks of their own and those of their family members that include math and computing. To help them get started, make a list of the following:

- measuring ingredients for recipes/cooking;

- estimating time for traveling from one place to another;

- making a budget; and

- spending money for food and other needs.

Tell students to describe how they use math to budget and count money, read a clock, keep score of a game, and solve problems. Encourage students to share their examples with the class.

4-2 READING AND WRITING, THEY'RE VITAL

Bobby is a seventh grader and really likes his math classes, but he doesn't see the purpose of taking language arts classes because he can read and talk with others just fine. Why should he take language arts classes seriously anyway? Describe at least two reasons.

SUGGESTED ANSWERS

(A) Language skills will help you communicate effectively with your co-workers.

(B) Language skills will help you understand what you read so that you can respond intelligently.

(C) Language skills will help you write so you can communicate through e-mail.

Summary: It is important to do well in English and language arts classes. When Bobby gets a job, he will need to be able to talk with his co-workers, read and understand information, and write. All of these skills are important for understanding reports, schedules, e-mail, and other forms of written communication. Quite often your written words will be someone's first impression of you. You must be able to read, write, and speak well to prove a point and communicate with people. For example, to work in a restaurant you need to read the menu and take orders; to be a chef, you have to read ingredients and follow directions; to be a lawyer, you have to read legal documents; and to be a police officer, you need to be able to write speeding tickets and generate police reports.

 The table on the next page lists careers that require strong reading and writing skills.

⊞ STATS OF NOTE

CAREER*	EDUCATION*	INCOME**
AUTHORS They develop original written content for advertisements, books, magazines, movie and television scripts, songs, and online publications.	BACHELOR'S DEGREE, LONG-TERM ON-THE-JOB TRAINING	$55,420
TECHNICAL WRITERS They produce instruction manuals and other documents to communicate information more easily.	BACHELOR'S DEGREE	$63,280
EDITORS They plan, review, and revise content for publication.	BACHELOR'S DEGREE	$51,470
PUBLIC RELATIONS SPECIALISTS They create and maintain a favorable public image for their employer. They write material for media releases, plan and direct public relations programs, and engage in fund raising.	BACHELOR'S DEGREE	$57,550
INTERPRETERS AND TRANSLATORS They change information from one language to another. Interpreters work in spoken or sign language, translators in written language.	BACHELOR'S DEGREE	$43,000

* Bureau of Labor Statistics, U.S. Department of Labor. Occupational Handbook, 2012–13 Edition
** Bureau of Labor Statistics, U.S. Department of Labor, Occupational Employment Statistics

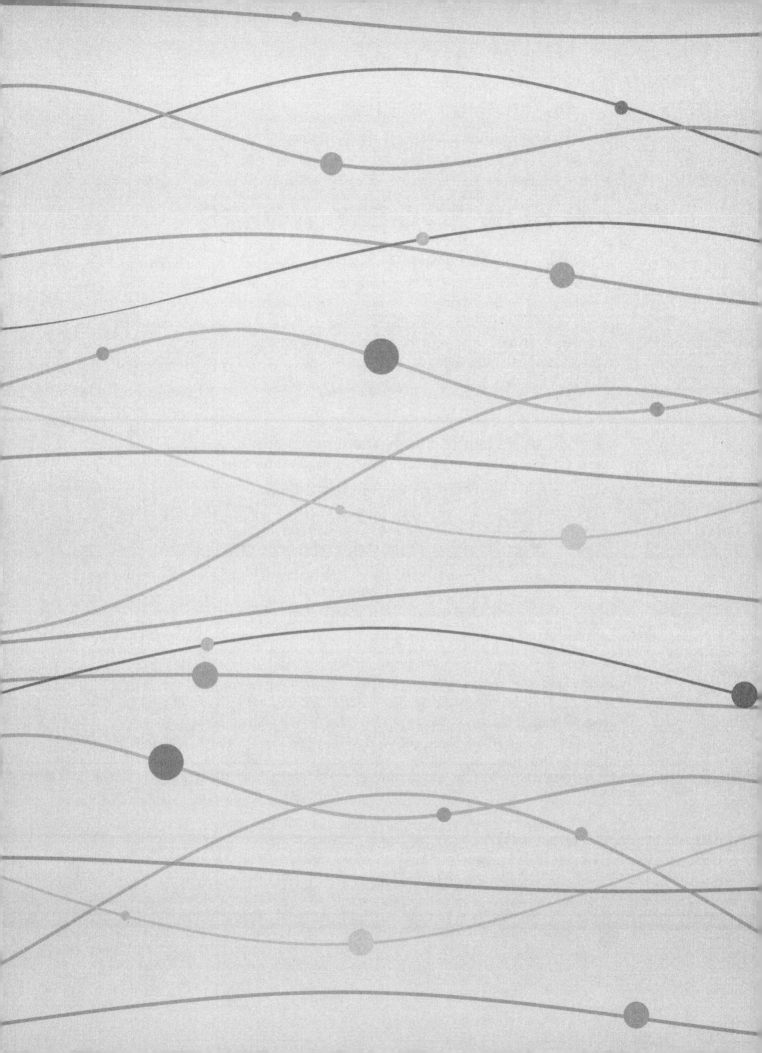

4-3 HOW SOCIETY WORKS

In social studies, we learn about how people live and interact with each other and how they have related to each other over time. This area of study also includes learning about cultural and political disagreements and the different ways that people work together to solve problems. Social studies and history also provide us with models for how communities develop and organize governments and other systems. In which of the following ways can you benefit from understanding social studies? (There may be more than one correct answer.)

✔ **A** Help you understand how your community works and how you can contribute in your community.

B Help you plan your next social event.

✔ **C** Help you understand people from other communities and countries and how your own identity and background are important.

Summary: We may not think of social studies this way, but social studies and history concepts are woven into everyday news and local events that shape our lives. The laws we follow, our election process, conflicts, and wars are all subjects of social studies. If you want to be the president of the United States, a teacher, a lawyer, a police officer, or a social worker, then you want to study and build skills in social studies and history.

 The table on the next page lists careers that require a strong background in history and social studies.

STATS OF NOTE

CAREER*	EDUCATION*	INCOME**
PUBLIC SERVANTS: ELECTED OFFICIALS, INCLUDING THE PRESIDENT, MAYOR, SENATORS They run all levels of government services, including local police and fire departments, towns and cities, and Congress.	DEPENDENT ON SERVICE TYPE (BA–ADVANCED)	DEPENDS ON SERVICE
SECONDARY TEACHERS They help students learn school subjects, develop knowledge and skills, and prepare for a career. Teachers play a big role in guiding students to become responsible adults.	BACHELOR'S DEGREE	$84,420
LAWYERS They research, determine, and apply the law. They give advice to people who need help with personal and business affairs.	BACHELOR'S DEGREE AND A LAW DEGREE	$113,240
POLICE OFFICERS (LOCAL GOVERNMENT) They protect people and their property. They write reports to record events and incidents from each day. They write tickets and communicate with people who break the law.	HIGH SCHOOL DIPLOMA AND AT LEAST ON-THE-JOB TRAINING	$53,210
SOCIAL SERVICE WORKERS They help people identify their needs and find resources. They help students find educational opportunities and jobs. They prevent homelessness and guide people to find health care and other services.	BACHELOR'S DEGREE	$39,960

* *Bureau of Labor Statistics, U.S. Department of Labor: Occupational Handbook, 2010–11 Edition.*
** *Bureau of Labor Statistics, U.S. Department of Labor, Occupational Employment Statistics.*

Will There Ever Be Peace?

Have students work in small groups. Provide them with copies of newspapers or magazines and have them research at least one major conflict in world news. Tell students to identify the source of the conflict. Then have them name other wars or conflicts from history (world wars, Iraq War, Vietnam War). Ask: Is it possible for nations and people to live peacefully, without war? Why or why not?

Ask students to debate whether it is possible to have a future in which countries do not fight wars.

4-4 SCIENCE TEACHES CRITICAL THINKING

Teachers should have you study science so that you understand living things and the world around you. True or false?

 **A** True   **B** False

Summary: The most important thing about science is not memorizing terms and facts; it is learning about the world and how it works. Scientific "facts" change every day as new discoveries are made. Science teaches you to think critically, research information, develop an argument based on facts, and learn to put your argument in written form. If you like science, you might like to work in environmental science, forensic science, marine biology, or meteorology. You could also work as a radiological (X-ray) technician or respiratory therapist or in many other areas of medical science.

  The table on the next page lists careers that require a background in science.

CAREER*	EDUCATION*	INCOME**
ENVIRONMENTAL SCIENTISTS They research the hazards that affect people and wildlife—and their environments. They study air, food, water, and soil to find ways to clean and protect the environment. In some cases, they write papers to explain their work to others.	BACHELOR'S DEGREE	$61,010
FORENSIC SCIENCE TECHNICIANS They investigate crimes by looking at and studying evidence. They usually analyze DNA, test weapons, or examine glass, hair, and other evidence found at the scene of a crime. They write reports on their findings and sometimes have to go to court and tell the court what they find out.	ASSOCIATE'S DEGREE OR A CERTIFICATION	$51,480
MARINE BIOLOGISTS They study saltwater plants and animals and what happens inside them. They work in science labs, go to the places where the plants and animals live to do field research, and write reports about what they learn. Some work on ships and scuba dive.	BACHELOR'S OR MASTER'S DEGREE	$66,510

STATS OF NOTE

CAREER*	EDUCATION*	INCOME**
METEOROLOGISTS They study the science of the atmosphere. Some predict the weather and provide weather forecasts. Others research the earth's climate.	BACHELOR'S DEGREE	$84,710
RADIOLOGICAL TECHNICIANS They work with patients and help them get in the correct position for X-rays.	ASSOCIATE'S DEGREE OR CERTIFICATION PROGRAM	$53,240
RESPIRATORY THERAPISTS They help people who have difficulty breathing or who have breathing disorders.	ASSOCIATE'S DEGREE	$53,330

* *Bureau of Labor Statistics, U.S. Department of Labor: Occupational Handbook, 2010–11 Edition.*
** *Bureau of Labor Statistics, U.S. Department of Labor, Occupational Employment Statistics.*

4-5 LANGUAGE INSIGHTS

Studying a foreign language (such as Spanish) can help you to better understand English. True or false?

 ✔Ⓐ True   Ⓑ False

Summary: When you study a foreign language, you learn the rhythm of the language and you fine-tune your English skills. Studying foreign languages helps you learn more about the everyday life of the people who live and work in the places where that language is spoken. Some jobs that require you to speak a language other than English include foreign-language teachers, international business executives, diplomats, and social workers. Even if you don't have a job that involves another language, when you travel to another country you can use a foreign language to communicate directly with the people of that country.

 The table on the next page lists careers that require strong reading and writing skills.

 STATS OF NOTE

CAREER*	EDUCATION*	INCOME**
FOREIGN LANGUAGE TEACHERS They teach languages and literature courses in languages other than English.	BACHELOR'S DEGREE	$59,630
INTERNATIONAL BUSINESS PROFESSIONALS They specialize in business dealings with companies overseas and usually manage analysts, administrative service managers.	BACHELOR'S DEGREE, MASTER'S DEGREE	$73,700***
FOREIGN SERVICE OFFICERS**** They are America's diplomatic corps. They typically are generalists who issue visas, protect U.S. citizens overseas, accompany foreign officials, report on diplomatic issues, and conduct press conferences for ambassadors.	BACHELOR'S DEGREE	$95,608
SOCIAL WORKERS They help people identify their needs and find resources. They help students find educational opportunities and jobs. They help prevent homelessness and guide people to find health care and other services.	BACHELOR'S DEGREE	$42,480

* Bureau of Labor Statistics, U.S. Department of Labor: Occupational Handbook, 2012–13 Edition.
** Bureau of Labor Statistics, U.S. Department of Labor, Occupational Employment Statistics.
*** U.S. Department of Labor, using median averages for 2008.
**** 2008–2012, Glassdoor. http://www.glassdoor.com

SUPPLEMENTAL DISCUSSION

Doing Well Opens Doors

Ask students to discuss the opportunities that come from performing
well in school.

Suggested answers:

A. Performing well in school offers you the opportunity to attend college or a
training program or get a good job. Remember, high academic performance (good
grades, a high grade point average) does not guarantee success. Adults stress that
you should study and excel because these abilities show that you are willing to
learn the material in order to succeed.

B. In school, you learn to read and write, which helps you communicate with
your family, friends, peers, and future co-workers. Although you may not think
about it, reading and writing are important in order to succeed and do well as you
grow up. How do you talk with your friends? How do you do things like e-mail,
blog, take notes in class, and text-message? What will most likely be your first line
of communication when you are applying for a job? You will have to fill out an
application form, develop a résumé and cover letter, or write an e-mail message to
the person who is hiring. The better you are at writing and explaining your skills,
the better chance you have of getting a good job.

C. The things you learn in school will help you when you grow up and live
in your own apartment or house. Math skills will help you pay your bills.
Social studies knowledge will help you understand your community and why
the political world is the way it is, and science will help you understand the
physical world around you.

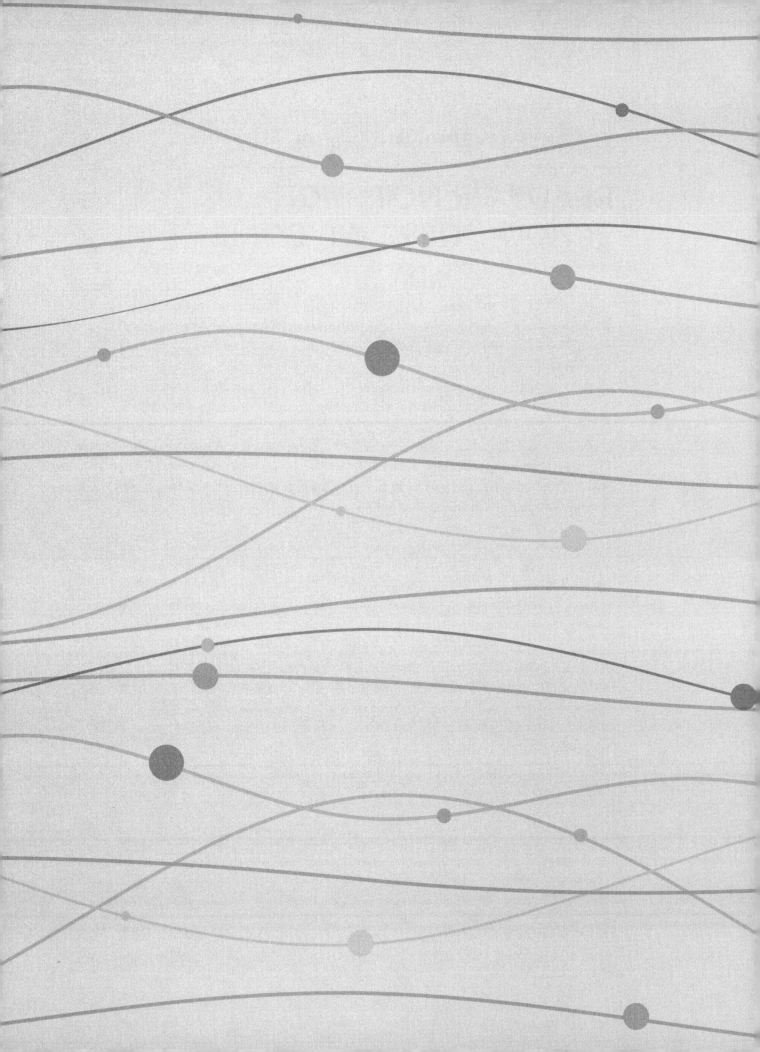

READY OR NOT: HIGH SCHOOL, HERE WE COME

"Ready or Not: High School, Here We Come" underscores for students that in order to have more choices and opportunities in life, they need to learn the material covered in middle school so that they can do well in high school. It helps adults guide students to focus on learning and getting good grades because high school is more challenging than middle school. In this section, students will learn suggestions for helping them prepare for high school. In a focus group conducted for this book, freshman students were asked, "What do you wish you had known about high school when you were in middle school?" The most common response was that they wished they had worked harder at learning and getting good grades in middle school because high school classes are more difficult than middle school classes.

It is important that we talk early with students about high school and the transition from middle school to high school. The tragic reality is that students who decide to drop out of or disengage from high school make this decision in the middle grades. There are many variables that young people use to determine whether they are going to drop out. Students decide to drop out of high school because of negative experiences such as difficult transition to high school, deficiency in basic skills, grade retention, or behavioral problems that begin before ninth grade.[30] As adults, we can help students make the transition to high school as seamless as possible. This section emphasizes that middle school is an important stepping-stone in life and that, though sometimes scary, high school is interesting and can be fun.

The section also provides basics such as the nomenclature for freshmen, sophomores, juniors, and seniors, and it continues the dialogue regarding what a person's life might look like if he or she doesn't graduate from high school. It presents facts regarding that in order to go to college students need to do well in high school, because colleges' admissions decisions are based on how well they do in high school. It identifies that not only are the admissions departments interested in high school grade-point averages, but that they are also interested in class rankings, standardized test scores, the level of difficulty of courses taken, and extracurricular activities in which students are involved.

 This icon identifies the material that can be downloaded and printed for students at **www.corwin.com/connectingthedots.**

5-1 PREPARE NOW FOR HARDER CLASSES

One hundred high school students were asked, "What do you wish you had known about high school when you were in middle school?" Out of the following responses, which one do you think was the most common response?

A I wish someone had told me where the drinking fountains were.

B I wish I knew that there was so much more homework in high school than middle school.

✔ C I wish someone had told me how serious I should have been about getting good grades and learning in middle school because high school classes are hard.

D I wish I knew that I would have to take a gym class.

TOPIC 5 | SUBJECT 1

Summary: The most common response was that students wished they had been told that they should be serious about getting good grades and learning in middle school because high school classes are difficult. You have to be serious about working hard in middle school to prepare yourself for high school classes. High school classes build on learning and skills from middle school classes, so you need to know the material from middle school in order to understand the material in high school.

EXTENSION ACTIVITY

How Can I Get Ready for High School?

Have students work with a partner. Tell them to make a list of what they can do to prepare for high school. To prompt their thinking, tell them to think about how middle school and high school are alike and different. As a class, discuss students' lists. Some possible responses: learning study habits, getting organized, and managing your time.

5-2 FRESHMAN, JUNIOR . . . WHAT'S THAT?

Tyler is a sophomore in high school, and he knows that he has to go to college or get training beyond high school in order to get a good job. Tyler struggles in school to get good grades, and his older sister, Tamron, recommended that he take Advanced Placement classes instead of College Prep classes to help him prepare for college. Is Tamron's advice true or false?

 Ⓐ True ✔Ⓑ False

Summary: Tamron's advice was wrong. If Tyler is truly struggling in school, he should consider taking College Prep courses. This is because an AP class is basically a college class offered in high school, so the work is more demanding than high school. Tyler would be better off taking a College Prep class because the course work will prepare him to enter college with a stronger foundation. AP classes are a great option for students who are ready for a faster-paced class. One advantage for students who pass the end-of-year AP test is they can earn college credit to many colleges. Remember to take challenging classes, for college admissions look at the level of difficulty of classes when they consider students for admission.

5-3 MAXIMIZE YOUR CHOICES

You need to work hard in high school in order to have more choices and opportunities after high school. True or false?

 **✓Ⓐ** True   **Ⓑ** False

Summary: True. In order to have more choices and opportunities after high school, you need to do well in school. Working hard now will give you more options in the future. It's important to focus on studying and getting the best grades that you can because high school is more challenging than middle school. Some things you can do to prepare for high school are to turn homework in on time, participate in class, and thoroughly complete your assignments so that you learn the material and are ready to tackle harder assignments when you get to high school. If you have questions or problems, you can talk to your teacher or guidance counselor.

EXTENSION ACTIVITY

What I Want to Do

Ask students to write two paragraphs about what they want to do after high school. Ask them what type of job they think they might like and what type of schooling they think they will need. Ask them if they will need to go to college, get on-the-job training, or go right to work.

5-4 HOW IMPORTANT IS IT, REALLY?

MJ is a freshman in high school and has a 2.0 grade-point average (GPA). That's a C average. MJ is having a hard time in school and is thinking about dropping out. He is worried about dropping out because he doesn't know what will happen if he does, so he decided to talk to his student counselor. His counselor told him some pretty scary statistics about what would likely happen to him if he dropped out of high school. Which of the follow are true? (There may be more than one correct answer.)

✔(A) High school dropouts have a harder time getting jobs than high school graduates.

✔(B) High school dropouts earn lower wages than high school graduates.

✔(C) High school dropouts are more likely to be involved in criminal activity.

Summary: All the statistics summarized by MJ's counselor are true. High school dropouts are more likely to be unemployed, earn lower wages, and be involved in criminal activity. In fact, over the course of his or her lifetime, a high school dropout earns, on average, about $260,000 less than a high school graduate.[31] MJ made a really good decision to talk with his counselor because he learned that there were other students who were also having a hard time in school and that school and life can sometimes be hard. MJ learned that if he didn't graduate from high school his life would be even harder, so he decided to stick with it and graduate.

If you are finding it difficult to get good grades, ask your teacher or a classmate for help. Sometimes the problems you are having are not as hard to solve as you think. When you seek help from a classmate, you might make a new friend. Make sure you talk to an adult if you are having problems because, believe it or not, adults were once middle school students too. They might have good advice.

5-5 HARDER CLASSES CARRY MORE WEIGHT

Bridget and Darren are high school seniors in the same school. They both volunteer at school and in the community. They got the same score on their standardized tests for college, and they both got A- averages in high school. Bridget and Darren also participated in extracurricular activities: Bridget played soccer and took dance classes and Darren played baseball and participated in band. Bridget, however, took harder classes. They both dreamed of going to the same college. Bridget was accepted, but Darren was not. Why do you think Bridget got chosen over Darren?

Ⓐ Colleges prefer soccer athletes more than baseball athletes.

✔Ⓑ Bridget took harder classes than Darren.

Ⓒ Colleges prefer band more than dance.

Ⓓ Bridget's parents had better jobs than Darren's parents.

Summary: Colleges are interested in all the things that Darren and Bridget did, but Bridget got chosen over Darren because Bridget took harder classes than Darren. The college saw that Bridget worked harder to get her A- average than Darren did. Colleges consider high school grade-point averages, class rankings, test scores for college, the difficulty of courses taken, and what you do outside of school. Make sure to be involved in the community during your free time. You can have a job or internship, volunteer in community events, or participate in student government, sports, band, or the arts. You should practice taking standardized tests; ask your teacher or school counselor how to do this.

An AP class is an advanced placement course offered in most high schools. AP classes allow you to earn college credit while you are in high school.

SUPPLEMENTAL DISCUSSION

Working Hard Leads to . . .

Ask students: Why should you work hard in high school? And what are some things you can do to make the most of the opportunities in high school?

Considerations:

A. In order to have more choices and opportunities after high school, you need to do your best in school. Working hard now will give you more options in the future.

B. It's important to focus on learning and getting good grades because high school is harder than middle school. Some things you can do so that you are ready for high school are to turn homework in on time, participate in class, and take time on your assignments so that you learn the material and are ready to tackle harder assignments when you get to high school.

C. If you have questions or problems, you can talk to your teacher or guidance counselor.

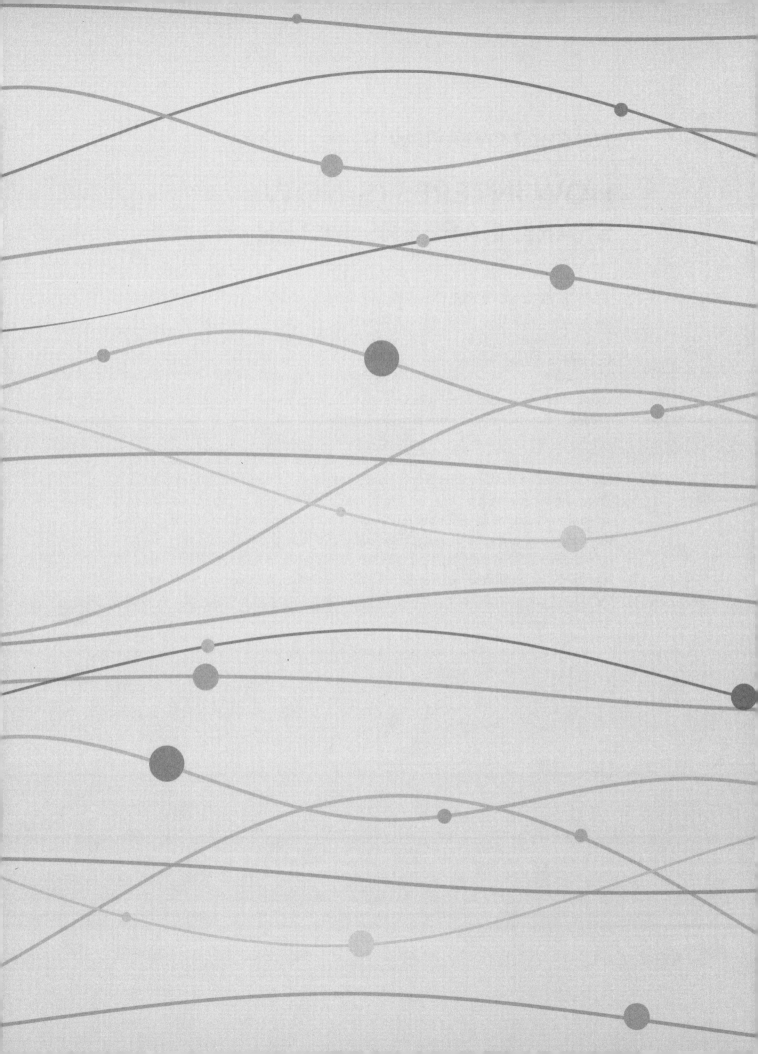

HOW INTERESTS NOW SPARK CAREERS LATER

"How Interests Now Spark Careers Later" helps students connect school subjects, the interests that they have, and the careers that align with their interests. This focus enables students to critically think about the types of jobs they might like and also that in order to get these jobs they need to focus on school and earn an education. This section points out to students that having an idea of careers that match their interests and abilities will allow them to make decisions about the job or career that they might want after high school.

When students develop an idea of what they want to do when they grow up, they take an interest in the subjects and classes they should focus on in high school. They also learn whether they need to go to college or seek additional training beyond high school for their chosen career. This prompts students to think about the things they are good at, what they enjoy, and how the skills that they have help them in school subjects. Students are prompted to act—as now is the time to start thinking, exploring and developing their interests. And yet, it's also okay if they don't know what they want to do when they grow up because people change their minds as they learn new things.

SUBJECTS COVERED IN THIS TOPIC

6-1   Let Interests Guide Educational Path

6-2   Interests Lead to Many Options

6-3   Sorting Out Job Titles

6-4   Lots of Careers in Health Care

6-5   Match Subjects to Interests

 This icon identifies the material that can be downloaded and printed for students at **www.corwin.com/connectingthedots.**

6-1 LET INTERESTS GUIDE EDUCATIONAL PATH

Will is in high school and is having a hard time deciding what he wants to do when he grows up. He likes helping people but doesn't think he wants to be a doctor because he isn't interested in chemistry (or blood, for that matter). Will made an appointment with his school counselor, who told him that if he earns his bachelor's degree in human services or social work, he can get a job and help others as a community service director, substance-abuse counselor, or volunteer coordinator. A college degree allows a person to enter many occupations that help people. True or false?

 **A** True   **B** False

Summary: True. A college degree enables individuals to enter many occupations that help people. Social work is a profession for people who have a desire to improve other people's lives. A person with a bachelor's degree in social work works directly with people or with policies and research that help people. Some jobs that a social worker might have are child, family, and school social worker, substance-abuse social worker, and volunteer coordinator. There are careers in many areas, and, as long as you know your interests and the skills you have, you can start thinking about what you want to do for a job or career.

 The table on the next page lists careers in social work.

STATS OF NOTE

CAREER*	EDUCATION*	INCOME**
CHILD, FAMILY, AND SCHOOL SOCIAL SERVICE WORKERS They provide social services and assistance to improve the social and emotional functioning of children and their families and to improve family well-being and academics of students.	BACHELOR'S DEGREE	$39,960
SUBSTANCE-ABUSE SOCIAL WORKERS They work with people who have eating disorders or are addicted to drugs, alcohol, or gambling. The counselors work to stop and prevent the addictive behaviors and work with families of people with addiction.	BACHELOR'S DEGREE	$38,500
VOLUNTEER COORDINATORS They usually work with organizations that use volunteers. Their job is to recruit volunteers, train volunteers, and place volunteers.	BACHELOR'S DEGREE	$36,000

* Bureau of Labor Statistics, U.S. Department of Labor. Occupational Handbook, 2010–11 Edition.
** Bureau of Labor Statistics, U.S. Department of Labor, Occupational Employment Statistics.

I'm Good at . . .

Ask students to write individual lists, noting their top five greatest skills and talents. Ask: What are you really good at? What are your talents? These can be anything from reading to swimming to playing video games to babysitting. Help the students connect how their talents might relate to a job and how some of their skills might be transferable from one job to another.

6-2 INTERESTS LEAD TO MANY OPTIONS

Felicia really likes fixing things and working on her computer. She told her mom this, and her mom said that when she is done with high school she should go to college to get a degree in computer science. Which of the following is something that Felicia probably would not do with a degree in computer science?

A Computer programming

B Technical support

✔**C** Food lab technician

Summary: If Felicia wants to use her degree in computer science, food lab technician is probably not something she would do with her degree. People who work in laboratories usually have a bachelor's degree in science. They talk with nutritionists, doctors, and hospital employees to develop food products. If you like meeting new people and creating new foods, you might like a job as a food lab technician. Computer science is quite different. Some things you would do with a degree in computer science include software engineer, computer systems analyst, web developer, computer support specialist, or computer programmer. It is a growing field, so there will continue to be lots of job openings in computer science. Most jobs require you to know how to use a computer, and if you have skills or are interested in computers or like fixing things, do some research on what types of jobs there are in computer science. You can earn a degree in computer science from a two-year or four-year college.

 The table on the next page lists careers that require a degree in computer science.

CAREER*	EDUCATION*	INCOME**
SOFTWARE ENGINEERS They develop, create, and modify general computer applications software or specialized utility programs. They also analyze user needs and develop software solutions.	BACHELOR'S DEGREE	$87,480
COMPUTER SYSTEMS ANALYSTS They analyze science, engineering, business, and all other data processing problems for application to electronic data processing systems.	BACHELOR'S DEGREE	$77,080
WEB DEVELOPERS They are responsible for the technical aspects of website creation. Using software languages and tools, they create applications for the Web.	BACHELOR'S DEGREE	$58,400
COMPUTER SUPPORT SPECIALISTS They provide technical assistance to computer system users. They answer questions or resolve computer problems for clients in person, via telephone, or from remote locations.	BACHELOR'S DEGREE	$44,300
COMPUTER PROGRAMMERS They convert project specifications and statements of problems and procedures to detailed logical flowcharts for coding into computer language.	ASSOCIATE'S DEGREE, BACHELOR'S DEGREE	$70,940

* Bureau of Labor Statistics, U.S. Department of Labor. Occupational Handbook, 2010–11 Edition.
** Bureau of Labor Statistics, U.S. Department of Labor, Occupational Employment Statistics.

6-3 SORTING OUT JOB TITLES

If you like to work with children, you might like a job as a coach, pediatrician, geriatrician, teacher, or nurse. True or false?

Summary: The answer is false. Tell students that all of these careers involve helping other people. If you like children and think you might like to work with them, you might like a job being a coach, pediatrician, teacher, or nurse, but probably not a geriatrician. "Geriatrician" is a fancy word for people who work with older adults. It's important for you to think about the things you like and find interesting. There are so many different types of jobs out there that if you can pinpoint your interests, you will be able to find a job that matches best with whatever your interests are. Ways to learn about what your interests are may include getting a job after school or in the summer, volunteering for a community event, or talking with or going to work with adults who have jobs that sound interesting. Colleges and employers are interested in applicants who have experience, so while uncovering your interests, you can also get ahead of others who are interested in the same positions just by working or volunteering in these areas to test them out.

Would I Like That Job?

Explain this saying to students: "When you have a job you love you will never work a day in your life." Ask students what they think this means. Explain that when you enjoy what you do, it may not always feel like work. Guide students to understand that most good jobs require focus, hard work, and commitment. And yet, if you enjoy what you do, it may not feel like work. Have students brainstorm and describe why it is important to be interested in whatever job they might get. Have them describe what it means to be interested in a job. Suggested talking points include enjoying co-workers, being challenged, and getting satisfaction from solving problems or helping people.

6-4 LOTS OF CAREERS IN HEALTH CARE

With a degree in the health care field, among the things you could be include a pharmacist, a registered nurse, or an art therapist. True or false?

 **✓Ⓐ True**   **Ⓑ False**

Summary: True. Pharmacist, registered nurse, and art therapist are just a few of the many possibilities in the health care field. If you are interested in helping people who are sick or need medical help, you might like a career in health care. If you think you would like to fill medication prescriptions for patients and tell them how much medicine they should take or how the medicine works in their bodies, you might like to be a pharmacist. This also means you have good skills working with detailed information. Pharmacists measure medications and treatments, and they must be very careful in their work. If you are interested in treating patients and teaching them about medical conditions and giving them emotional support, you might want to be a nurse or doctor. If you enjoy art, you could be an art therapist and use art supplies such as crayons and paints to help people communicate their feelings so that you can help them. The health care field is growing, and this means that when you graduate from high school, college, or a training program, there will likely be job openings.[32] Start thinking about what you like to do and what you are interested in. You are more likely to complete your education or training program if you have thought about career choices that interest you. Both two-year and four-year colleges have programs in the health care field.

»W The table on the next page lists careers in health care.

CAREER*	EDUCATION*	INCOME**
PHARMACISTS They dispense drugs prescribed by physicians and other health practitioners and provide information to patients about medications and their use.	DOCTOR OF PHARMACY	$109,180
REGISTERED NURSES They assess patient health problems and needs, develop and implement nursing care plans, and maintain medical records.	ASSOCIATE'S DEGREE, BACHELOR'S DEGREE	$63,750
ART THERAPISTS They use art supplies such as crayons and paints to help people communicate their feelings so that they can be helped.	BACHELOR'S DEGREE	$39,440
OCCUPATIONAL THERAPIST AIDES They work with an occupational therapist or occupational therapy assistant to perform only delegated, selected, or routine tasks in specific situations.	ASSOCIATE'S DEGREE	$25,730
PHYSICAL THERAPIST ASSISTANTS They assist physical therapists in providing physical therapy treatments and procedures.	ASSOCIATE'S DEGREE	$48,290

* Bureau of Labor Statistics, U.S. Department of Labor. Occupational Handbook, 2010–11 Edition.
** Bureau of Labor Statistics, U.S. Department of Labor, Occupational Employment Statistics.

6-5 MATCH SUBJECTS TO INTERESTS

Andrés really likes solving story problems and puzzles, and he likes figuring out the correct answers to interesting questions. He enjoys all of his classes equally. What school subjects do you think will help Andrés develop his problem-solving skills? (There may be more than one correct answer.)

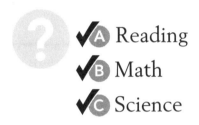

✔ Ⓐ Reading

✔ Ⓑ Math

✔ Ⓒ Science

Summary: Reading, math, and science will help Andrés develop his problem-solving skills. If you think math is challenging but you like solving problems, keep working to improve your math skills and ask your teacher or a tutor for help. Remember that sometimes your interests won't match what you are best at, but most of the time skills can be learned in your interest area. It's really important that you're interested in what you want to be so that you enjoy your education and training. If you earn a bachelor's degree in math, you can be an accountant, an insurance agent, a financial analyst, or even an economist. When planning for your future education or training, make sure that the college or training program offers programs that you're interested in. Once you get to college, you will get to choose the classes that you take.

»Ⓦ The table on the next page lists careers that require strong math skills.

CAREER*	EDUCATION*	INCOME**
ARCHITECTS They draw and design homes, buildings, parks, and other structures. They are trained to develop the idea of what a structure will look like and turn the idea into images for clients to look at and builders to use to build the structure.	BACHELOR'S DEGREE	$72,700
ASTRONAUT* ** They command or pilot spacecraft and work in space.	BACHELOR'S DEGREE, 3 YEARS' EXPERIENCE, ADVANCED DEGREE	$65,140
FINANCIAL ANALYSTS They help individuals, families, and businesses make decisions about how to save and invest their money.	BACHELOR'S DEGREE	$73,670
ECONOMISTS They collect and consider, data and look for trends in the economy. They also research how society distributes land, work, social services, and machinery to produce goods and services.	BACHELOR'S DEGREE, MASTER'S DEGREE	$86,930

* Bureau of Labor Statistics, U.S. Department of Labor. Occupational Handbook, 2010–11 Edition.
** Bureau of Labor Statistics, U.S. Department of Labor, Occupational Employment Statistics.
*** NASA Website- http://www.nasa.gov/home/index.html

SUPPLEMENTAL DISCUSSION

Decisions, Decisions . . .

Ask students to describe some strategies to use when deciding on a career.

Suggested answers:

A. Skills and interests assessment: Give some thought to what you are good at and what you like to do and are interested in.

B. Interests and relationship to jobs: Think about what you are interested in and whether this interest is related to a career. Sometimes your interest won't match your skills, but in most cases skills can be learned in your interest area.

C. Opportunity: Education beyond high school opens doors and opportunities. You can find work you enjoy doing every day and earn money along the way.

D. Job availability: Consider the jobs and skills that employers are looking for to help identify the industries that are hiring so that you can gain knowledge and skills in those fields and increase your chances of being hired.

NAVIGATING TO THE JOB OF YOUR DREAMS

"Navigating to the Job of Your Dreams" focuses students' attention on planning for the amount of education that they will need and the types of colleges or training programs that are available for a particular career field. This section helps adults talk with students and emphasize that most employers require a high school diploma. This section also focuses on the fact that in the future most careers and jobs are likely to require some education or training after high school. The questions in this section exemplify that there are careers that require bachelor's degrees or more, but many will require two or fewer years of education after high school.

This section provides examples of the types of questions that students should ask themselves as they begin the journey of planning their educational and career pathways. It points out that as students map out their careers they need to consider what jobs are in demand so that once they have completed college they will be able to find a job in their chosen field.

SUBJECTS COVERED IN THIS TOPIC

7-1   Becoming Well-Rounded

7-2   Job Requirements Are Getting Tougher

7-3   Becoming a Professional Athlete

7-4   Alternatives to a Four-Year Degree

7-5   What Can I Do With a Two-Year Degree?

7-1 BECOMING WELL-ROUNDED

Employers make hiring decisions based only on grades and how long you have been in school. True or false?

  Ⓐ True ✔Ⓑ False

Summary: False. Employers want educated employees who have transferable skills, such as communication skills, honesty/integrity, motivation/initiative, a strong work ethic, teamwork skills, computer skills, analytical skills, flexibility/adaptability, organizational skills, and leadership skills.[33] Transferable skills are those skills that aren't specific to a particular job or occupation, but instead are useful in many jobs as well as in your daily life. So in addition to studying hard, you should work to develop these additional skills. Fortunately, the development of these skills is usually through fun and social activities. You can work on these skills simply by joining a team or a club or getting a job or internship. Volunteering and participating in performing arts are other ways to learn and to practice working with others.

Employers Want Employees Who . . .

Have students work in small groups. Tell them to discuss the following careers: fire fighter; doctor; store owner. Then ask students to describe why the following skills are important in these careers: communication skills, honesty/integrity, motivation/initiative, a strong work ethic, teamwork skills, computer skills, analytical skills, flexibility/adaptability, organizational skills, and leadership skills. Tell students to write a total of three examples of these skills as they are used in these three careers. Ask: If you were looking for a job at the fire department, at a doctor's office or hospital, or at a store, why would these skills be important to the employers?

7-2 JOB REQUIREMENTS ARE GETTING TOUGHER

Lucy is a high school sophomore and starting to think about what she wants to do when she grows up and if she will need to go to college or get special training to work in the field that she's considering. Her high school counselor told her that by the year 2018, seven of the 10 fastest-growing occupations will require two-year degrees or on-the-job training.[34] Why do you think that future occupations will require education beyond high school?

SUGGESTED ANSWERS

A Changes in technology and computers.

B Globalization and the need to communicate with the rest of the world.

C There will be a need for "green" jobs— people who work in energy conservation and environmental preservation.

D Employers seek workers with good skill sets.

Summary: Future occupations will require education beyond high school because there will continue to be upgrades and changes in technology and the way the world does business. The counselor wants Lucy to consider that she will likely need education or training beyond high school so that when she graduates from whatever program she chooses there will be job openings in her chosen field. In many cases, a two-year associate's degree can lead to well-paying jobs and may be all you need for your desired career. Jobs that require an associate's degree include nurse, forensic or ballistics crime-scene investigator, computer technician, police officer, solar-panel installer, and MRI repair person. Consider "green jobs" in the clean energy field because these career areas are growing.

Globalization: is how we describe the trend in our world for economies (finances) and societies (people and politics) to become integrated through communications, imports, and exports.

Green Jobs: green jobs are jobs that improve or preserve the environment. Green jobs can be found in many different career areas, such as agriculture, manufacturing, and research and development (R&D).

7-3 BECOMING A PROFESSIONAL ATHLETE

Peyton is a ninth grader and on the varsity basketball team. He is 6'7" and has the most rebounds and points on his team. Peyton earns good enough grades to pass his classes and play on the team. He isn't worried about academic achievement because he already has college scouts who are recruiting him to go to their colleges. Peyton does not need to worry about his GPA, and instead he can focus on basketball because he will probably go to college and be drafted into the NBA. True or false?

 **A** True ✔**B** False

Summary: False. Peyton is wrong to focus only on basketball. In fact, of all high school students who play a major sport, only about one out of 5,000 becomes a professional athlete. Many professional athletes don't earn enough money to make ends meet. The median annual income for this career is $40,210, many make less than $25,000, and few make millions of dollars.[35] It's great to be involved in sports because you develop communication and teamwork skills; just make sure you have a backup plan in case you don't become a professional athlete. Additionally, although still difficult to obtain, you might be able to get a scholarship to help you pay for college. Be sure to concentrate on earning a high GPA because you will need a good GPA to succeed in college classes. Regardless, even professional athletes will need to earn an education because they will need a job after their athletic career is over. This is because many athletes are professionals for a few years only. Some get too old, and some get injured.

I Think a Good Job for Me Would Be . . .

Ask the students to complete the sentence *I think a good job for me would be . . .* and write down at least five jobs they think they might want after high school or college. Ask them to list as many as they can think of, including interesting jobs that they have heard about. Ask students to share what they wrote down and discuss why they think the jobs they listed sound interesting.

7-4 ALTERNATIVES TO A FOUR-YEAR DEGREE

Damen is in a welder apprenticeship program, which is a combination of on-the-job training and classroom work. He is learning all the components that make up his highly skilled job. Damen had other options for apprenticeships. Of the following occupations, which of the following jobs are offered as apprenticeships at a community college? (There may be more than one correct answer.)

✔ Ⓐ Electrician

Ⓑ Interior Designer

✔ Ⓒ Machinist

Ⓓ Substance Abuse Social Worker

Summary: Damen could have done an apprenticeship to become an electrician or machinist. To become a substance-abuse social worker or an interior designer, you will need a bachelor's degree. There are many occupations that you can enter through an apprenticeship or community college. Usually you need to be hired first, and then your employer will connect you with an apprenticeship. If you think you would like to get technical on-the-job training while you are learning about your career, you should talk with your school counselor or contact your local community college. Apprenticeships and on-the-job training can lead to jobs with average earnings similar to those of people with bachelor's degrees. For example, an apprenticeship is required to become an electrician, and a bachelor's degree is required to become an interior designer, but the average annual earnings for both is about $47,000.[36]

 The table on the next page lists careers that require a high school diploma and additional education or training.

STATS OF NOTE

CAREER*	EDUCATION*	INCOME**
ELECTRICIANS They install, maintain, and repair electrical wiring, equipment, and fixtures.	APPRENTICESHIP	$47,180
INTERIOR DESIGNERS They plan, design, and furnish interiors of residential, commercial, or industrial buildings.	BACHELOR'S DEGREE	$46,180
MACHINISTS They set up and operate a variety of machine tools to produce precision parts.	APPRENTICESHIP, VOCATIONAL SCHOOLS, OR TECHNICAL OR COMMUNITY COLLEGE	$37,650
SUBSTANCE-ABUSE SOCIAL WORKERS They work with people who have eating disorders or are addicted to drugs, alcohol, or gambling. The counselors work to stop and prevent the addictive behaviors and work with families of people with addiction.	BACHELOR'S DEGREE	$38,500

Bureau of Labor Statistics, U.S. Department of Labor. Occupational Handbook, 2010–11 Edition.
**Bureau of Labor Statistics, U.S. Department of Labor, Occupational Employment Statistics.*

7-5 WHAT CAN I DO WITH A TWO-YEAR DEGREE?

Jalen knows how important getting additional education or training is after high school and wants to know what types of careers require a two-year (associate's) degree before he decides whether he will work toward an associate's degree or a bachelor's degree after high school. Which of the following fields of study do you think was one of the top associate's degrees in demand in 2010?

✔Ⓐ Computer support specialist

Ⓑ Education

Ⓒ Crime-scene investigation

Summary: Jalen learned that legal assistants, registered nurses, and computer support specialists are all top two-year degrees demanded by employers as of 2010.[37] Jalen is really interested in the law and didn't know that he could go to school after high school for two years (instead of four) to get a degree to become a legal assistant. Remember to consider the jobs and skills that are in demand to help identify the industries that are hiring so that you can get the skills in those fields to increase your chances of getting a job after college. This doesn't mean that you should consider only the skills that are most demanded by employers; you also need to consider your skills, what you are interested in doing, and what you want to do for your career.

 The table on the next page lists careers with strong job opportunities and that require associate's degrees.

STATS OF NOTE

CAREER*	EDUCATION*	INCOME**
LEGAL ASSISTANTS They help lawyers prepare for closings, hearings, trials, and meetings. They might investigate the facts of cases and make sure that all relevant information is considered.	ASSOCIATE'S DEGREE	$46,980
REGISTERED NURSES They assess patient health problems and needs, develop and implement nursing care plans, and maintain medical records. They administer nursing care to ill, injured, convalescent, and/or disabled patients.	ASSOCIATE'S DEGREE, BACHELOR'S DEGREE	$63,750
COMPUTER SUPPORT SPECIALISTS They work with businesses and help people who have problems with their computers and manage computer network security.	ASSOCIATE'S DEGREE	$44,300
AEROSPACE ENGINEERING AND OPERATIONS TECHNICIANS They operate, install, adjust, and maintain computer/ communications systems, and other data tests to launch, track, position, and evaluate air and space vehicles. They may record and interpret test data.	ASSOCIATE'S DEGREE	$56,960

CAREER*	EDUCATION*	INCOME**
FASHION DESIGNERS They study fashion trends, draw new clothing designs, select colors and fabrics, and oversee the creation process.	ASSOCIATE'S DEGREE	$64,260
MRI (MAGNETIC RESONANCE IMAGING) TECHNICIANS They perform diagnostic imaging examinations. They perform imaging examinations like x-rays.	ASSOCIATE'S DEGREE	$53,240

Bureau of Labor Statistics, U.S. Department of Labor. Occupational Handbook, 2010–11 Edition.
**Bureau of Labor Statistics, U.S. Department of Labor, Occupational Employment Statistics.*

SUPPLEMENTAL DISCUSSION

Is College the Right Choice?

Gabe isn't sure what he wants to do when he grows up, but he thinks that whatever he wants to do will require at least some education or training beyond high school. What are some reasons a mentor might advise Gabe that investing in education beyond high school (even if he doesn't know what he wants to do for a career) is a good idea? Why is it important for Gabe to narrow down ideas about what he wants to do once he enrolls in college or a training program?

Suggested answers:
(in favor of attending college and narrowing the field of ideas regarding what you want to do):

A. Many job openings require a degree or certificate just to be considered for the job. In many cases, having your degree will be your "foot in the door" and will give you more options when you are looking for a job.

B. Attending a community college or four-year school can help you narrow down your interests and find a career that you enjoy. The school you attend and the classes you take after high school will offer projects and real-life opportunities, such as internships and jobs. You will have the opportunity to try out an area and get real-life experience.

C. Having a degree will open up opportunities for you. Schools have connections with employers, teachers, professors, and career-placement offices. These opportunities will help you look critically at different jobs and choose a career path that you will enjoy. Narrowing down the field of career choices will help you focus your studies, save money, graduate on time, and gain employment.

Continued on next page . . .

SUPPLEMENTAL DISCUSSION
(CONTINUED)

Suggested answers:
(in favor of not attending college without knowing what you want to do):

A. If you don't know what you want to focus on in college, you may end up switching your major, or area of study. In many cases, this will mean that you have to pay for extra classes and go to college for a longer period of time.

B. Many people who go to college without a plan end up dropping out of college, thereby spending time and money and not obtaining a degree.

C. You may find out that what you want to do doesn't require a college education. It may be the case that you need technical skills or apprenticeship training.

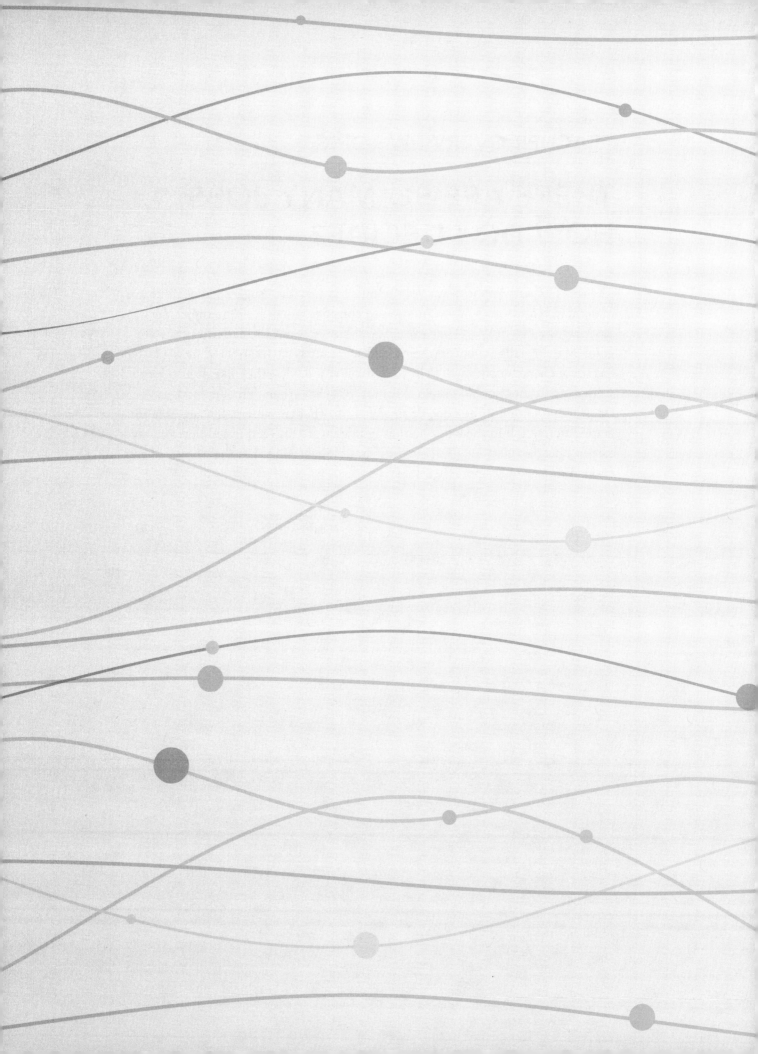

THERE ARE SO MANY JOBS. HOW DO I DECIDE?

The topic "There Are So Many Jobs. How Do I Decide?" suggests that there are many different sources of information to consider when deciding the careers students want to pursue: They should take into account the activities they are good at, their skills, what they enjoy, and what interests them. Finding a job that has these characteristics will help students find jobs that they like. It also reminds students that they should obtain skills for jobs that are in demand and that are transferable so that if they decide they want to change careers they are able to get a different job in the labor market. Students are also reminded that whatever career path they decide to follow, they should make sure that that they will earn enough money to support their lifestyle.

This section introduces students to an array of careers, underscoring the fact that there are many, many jobs that they might enjoy. Many students are unaware of the fact there are thousands of jobs in the labor market because they have never been introduced to them. Students are familiar with police officers, fire fighters, teachers, and doctors because they interact with these professions and are taught about these careers. On the other hand, students are not familiar with jobs such as computer programmer, engineer, wildlife biologist, and designer because they have not been introduced to these jobs.

SUBJECTS COVERED IN THIS TOPIC

8-1   Job Satisfaction Is More Than Money

8-2   Consider Your Interests, Favorite Subjects

8-3   Computer Skills Are Handy in Many Ways

8-4   Are You a CEO in the Making?

8-5   Improve Your Odds

 This icon identifies the material that can be downloaded and printed for students at **www.corwin.com/connectingthedots.**

8-1 JOB SATISFACTION IS MORE THAN MONEY

Ben wants to like the job he gets when he grows up, just as his dad does. Ben has friends who have parents who don't like their jobs, and he thinks it would be terrible not to like what he does most days of his life. Ben's dad works in human services. He tells Ben that in his job he helps people and that his work makes him feel good. In which of the following jobs would Ben be able to help people? (There is more than one correct answer.)

✔️Ⓐ Social worker

✔️Ⓑ Librarian

✔️Ⓒ Emergency and relief worker

✔️Ⓓ Nanny

Summary: All of them! Jobs in which you can help people are described as human services and include librarian, fitness trainer, mental and public health social worker, customer service representative, financial advisor, and more. As you can see from this list, there are all types of careers in human services. To be successful in the human service field, you should focus on developing communication, science, and technical skills.[38]

 The table on the next page lists careers in human services.

CAREER*	EDUCATION*	INCOME**
LIBRARIANS They help people do research, and they categorize materials.	MASTER'S DEGREE	$53,710
FITNESS TRAINERS They instruct or coach groups or individuals in exercise activities and the fundamentals of sports.	CERTIFICATION (MANY TIMES BACHELOR'S DEGREE)	$30,670
MENTAL AND PUBLIC HEALTH SOCIAL SERVICE WORKERS They provide persons, families, or vulnerable populations with the psychosocial support needed to cope with chronic, acute, or terminal illnesses.	BACHELOR'S DEGREE	$46,300
CUSTOMER SERVICE REPRESENTATIVES They interact with customers to provide information in response to inquiries about products and services, and to handle and resolve complaints.	ON-THE-JOB TRAINING, ASSOCIATE'S DEGREE, BACHELOR'S DEGREE	$30,290

CAREER*	EDUCATION*	INCOME**
PERSONAL FINANCIAL ADVISORS They advise clients on financial plans, utilizing knowledge of tax and investment strategies, securities, insurance, pension plans, and real estate.	BACHELOR'S DEGREE	$68,200

* *Bureau of Labor Statistics, U.S. Department of Labor: Occupational Handbook, 2010–11 Edition.*
** *Bureau of Labor Statistics, U.S. Department of Labor, Occupational Employment Statistics.*

Human Service Jobs

Remind students that human service jobs involve helping people. Ask students to identify other types of human service jobs.

8-2 CONSIDER YOUR INTERESTS, FAVORITE SUBJECTS

Christina is in middle school, and her family has a dog. She loves to take care of her dog and likes to watch *Animal Planet* on TV because it has shows with animals in them. Christina also likes her math and science classes and looks forward to taking biology and chemistry in high school. Considering her interests, which of the following careers might be a good match for Christina? (There may be more than one correct answer.)

A Computer programmer

✔B Wildlife biologist

C Engineer

✔D Veteranarian

Summary: Veterinarian or wildlife biologist would be good choices for Christina. Becoming a wildlife biologist would require at least a bachelor's degree, and becoming a veterinarian would require up to eight years of education beyond high school. Another option for Christina is to go to school for two years after high school to become a veterinary technician. She could even go to a technical school where she would be introduced to working with animals. There are many different careers that involve working with animals. To prepare for these careers, make sure you take health science and biology classes.

8-3 COMPUTER SKILLS ARE HANDY IN MANY WAYS

Julian is in middle school, and he likes to play on his computer. His grandmother was at his house and told him that she has never been on a computer and doesn't know how to type. Julian offered to teach his grandmother how to use the Internet and how to sign up for an e-mail account. Julian and his grandmother met once a week to work on the computer, and Julian loved it. He has decided that he wants to work with computers and thinks he wants to focus on building his career in the information technology (IT) field in the future. Which of the following career areas have opportunities for people with IT skills? (There is more than one correct answer.)

✔Ⓐ Financial services

✔Ⓑ Medical services

✔Ⓒ Environmental services

✔Ⓓ Design

Summary: Julian could get a job in financial services, medical services, environmental services, or design. Careers in IT can be found in almost every industry, so going to college or getting additional IT training after high school will give you a lot of career options. Make sure to develop transferable skills so that you can get a job in financial services working on Web design, and later switch jobs and do Web design for environmental services. Examples of transferable skills include listening, creating and communicating ideas, gathering information, and setting goals.

Another Possibility

Ask students to talk about the additional career fields Julian might consider if he likes helping his grandmother, and he has skills for helping people with computers. (He might like a human services career, helping others.) Encourage students to also think of careers in which problem solving is a good skill.

Ask: Why is problem solving a good skill for working in the IT field?

8-4 ARE YOU A CEO IN THE MAKING?

Pedro is a junior in high school and doesn't know what he wants to do when he grows up. He knows that he wants to go to college so that he can make enough money to be able to pay his bills and enjoy fun trips, but he doesn't know which career he wants after college. Pedro loves sports, is a good leader, and likes to organize people and to develop ideas. What career focus area do you think would be a good fit for Pedro?

Ⓐ Science/technology

✔**Ⓑ** Business management and administration

Ⓒ Communications

Ⓓ Food and natural resources

Summary: Pedro would most likely enjoy working in business management and administration. He can continue to develop his interests and skills by taking math, language arts, and business management classes. There are jobs in management and administration in almost every field, so when he has a better idea of his interests, he can focus on his particular field of interest. Jobs in management exist in many fields because many skills that are learned in business management college courses are relevant across many jobs. Pedro should also be sure to develop transferable skills, or skills that aren't specific to a particular job or occupation, but instead are useful in many jobs as well as in daily life. Some of these skills include, but are not limited to, being detail oriented, managing people and ideas, and making decisions. If Pedro gets his bachelor's degree in this area, he could become a public relations specialist, meeting and convention planner or management analyst.[39]

»W The table on the next page lists careers in business management.

STATS OF NOTE

CAREER*	EDUCATION*	INCOME**
PUBLIC RELATIONS SPECIALISTS They engage in promoting or creating good will for individuals, groups, or organizations by writing or selecting favorable publicity material and releasing it through various communications media.	BACHELOR'S DEGREE	$51,960
MEETING AND CONVENTION PLANNERS They coordinate activities of staff and convention personnel to make arrangements for group meetings and conventions.	ASSOCIATE'S DEGREE TO BACHELOR'S DEGREE	$44,780
MANAGEMENT ANALYSTS They conduct organizational studies and evaluations and design systems and procedures to assist management in operating more efficiently and effectively.	BACHELOR'S DEGREE	$75,250
SPORTS MANAGERS They manage, negotiate with, and lead people. They work with athletes to help them find the best team to play for, negotiate contracts, and help them get pay raises. Sports managers must know business and sports.	BACHELOR'S DEGREE	$50,000

* Bureau of Labor Statistics, U.S. Department of Labor: Occupational Handbook, 2010–11 Edition.
** Bureau of Labor Statistics, U.S. Department of Labor, Occupational Employment Statistics.

8-5 IMPROVE YOUR ODDS

Michelle has decided that she is going to go to college after high school to get her bachelor's degree. Her counselor has told her to make sure that her bachelor's degree is in an area that has a lot of jobs that businesses are hiring for. Her counselor wanted to make sure that the skills she learned would be in demand by businesses so it would be easier for her to find a well-paying job when she graduates with a bachelor's degree. Which of the following degrees do you think was most in demand in 2007, 2008, and 2009?

A Biology

B Political science

✔**C** Computer science

Summary: In recent years, computer science has been one of the top ten degrees that many businesses are seeking. There will continue to be employers looking for skilled people with computer science degrees. The top ten degrees in demand include the following:[40]

1. Accounting
2. Mechanical engineering
3. Electrical engineering
4. Computer Science
5. Business Administration/Management
6. Economics/Finance
7. Information Sciences & Systems
8. Computer Engineering
9. Management Information Systems
10. Marketing/Marketing Management

Taking into consideration the jobs and skills that are in demand can help you figure out what industries are hiring so that you can study (or major in) those fields to increase your chances of being hired after you graduate from your college or training program.

SUPPLEMENTAL DISCUSSION

So *This* Is Why I Need an Education

Ask students: "Why do you think certain jobs require education beyond high school even though the education might not seem necessary?"

Suggested answers:

A. In college, unlike high school, you choose a major and focus a lot of your learning in that field or major. Because of this specialized training, the employer knows that you have an understanding of the career area.

B. Employers like to see that people are willing to work hard, so going to college or getting into a training program shows an employer that you are a hard worker. It shows motivation and initiative.

C. Our world is constantly changing. The job you start with is likely to change in the future, even if you are working for the same employer. Training and education are lifelong, so knowing how to learn is a valuable life skill, and you practice this in college.

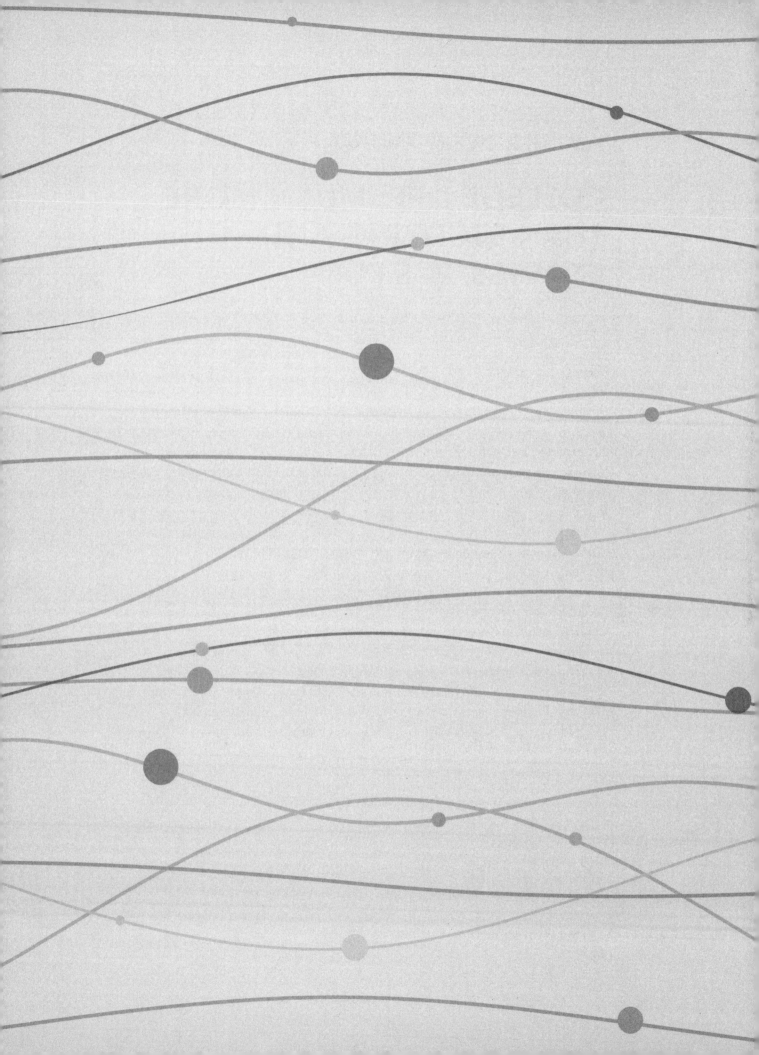

COLLEGE LIFE: MUCH MORE THAN STUDYING AND CLASSES, IT'S FUN!

"College Life: Much More Than Studying and Classes, It's Fun!" highlights that there are more than 4,000 colleges and universities, and they vary by size, diversity, and curriculum. Education beyond high school is one key to economic opportunity and is becoming increasingly important in the twenty-first century labor market. Obtaining an associate's degree, bachelor's degree, or training certificate will lead to increased earnings and helps individuals find a job and remain employed. Investing in postsecondary education takes time and a lot of planning by students and adults. This effort is well worth it because a college education and training provide students with the knowledge and skills students will use over the course of their lives to help them succeed. This section familiarizes students with college life to generate excitement and inform students about the types of colleges so that students will begin thinking about their own educational path.

Many high school students cannot imagine what it's like to go to college, and this topic helps adults educate, inform, and excite students about college life. Some students can't imagine what going to college is like because they don't have family members who have attended college and can talk with them about it. Other students think it sounds scary because they will have to move away from home. This section draws attention to the fact that there are many schools to choose from, so students can choose a school that is right for them. It reminds students that they should consider schools that match their interests and goals. The material in this section also introduces students to the idea that college is a time to focus on academics and decide the career area that they want to pursue, but it is also a good time to socialize, meet new people, and have fun.

SUBJECTS COVERED IN THIS TOPIC

9-1   Many Colleges to Choose From

9-2   More Time to Explore

9-3   New Experiences on the Horizon

9-4   How to Choose a College

9-5   More Than Hitting the Books

 This icon identifies the material that can be downloaded and printed for students at **www.corwin.com/connectingthedots.**

COLLEGE LIFE: MUCH MORE THAN STUDYING
AND CLASSES, IT'S FUN!

9-1 MANY COLLEGES TO CHOOSE FROM

About how many colleges and universities are there in the United States?

 A 2,600 **B** 3,400 ✔**C** 4,300

Summary: Can you believe that there are 4,314 degree-granting colleges and universities in the United States?[41] You probably can't name more than 20. In fact, most people don't recognize the majority of the school names. The great thing about there being so many schools is that there are a lot of schools to choose from and you will be able to find one that best matches what you like to do, your skills, your interests, and your goals.

EXTENSION ACTIVITY

List Them

Ask students to make a list of up to 20 colleges and universities. Ask them to share how they know about them. Ask: Did you learn about the names of these schools from family? From friends? Encourage students to also think about any information they know about the colleges and universities on their list. For example: Where is the campus? What do they know about the academics or sports programs?

9-2 MORE TIME TO EXPLORE

Charlie is in tenth grade (a sophomore). He isn't sure what type of job he wants when he grows up. Charlie needs to know what he wants to do before he goes to college because once he gets to college, he won't be able to change his mind. True or false?

 Ⓐ True ✔**Ⓑ** False

Summary: False. Charlie doesn't have to know now what he wants to do when he grows up to make a decision about college. However, the sooner he focuses on an area of study, the sooner he will graduate. Also, if his studies are focused he will save money. (Students who take five years to complete college pay more than students who take the traditional four-year period.) Charlie is like many students. A lot of students go to college and don't know what they want to be their first year. Most colleges don't make you decide what you want to focus on until the end of your second year in college. If you are like Charlie and aren't sure what you want to do, that's OK, but set a deadline for yourself, and set goals. Take the time to meet with your counselor in high school because he or she can help you decide what type of education or training program you should pursue. In college you will have a student advisor who will help you decide what type of job or career you might like based on your skills and interests. The great thing about high school and college is that there is always an adult who can help you make decisions about all the opportunities that are ahead of you.

THAT'S A GREAT IDEA FOR ME!

9-3 NEW EXPERIENCES ON THE HORIZON

Jayden's dad likes to tease Jayden. A couple of weeks ago they were talking about college, and Jayden asked his dad what it was like. His dad told him that it's really fun because you get to meet new people, watch sports and other games, and hang out with your friends. His dad also said it was great when he went to college because it was the first time he lived on his own and he didn't have to tell his parents what he was doing all the time. Jayden couldn't believe it when he found out that students live in dormitories where they sometimes have roommates, they didn't know before going to college. When you go to college you might have a roommate you didn't know before going to college. True or false?

 **✔A** True   **B** False

Summary: It's true. Jayden's dad is right. Many college students live in dorms (dormitories) and have roommates whom they didn't know before going to college. Living in a dorm is really fun because you get to live with a lot of people your age. Even though it's fun, you still have to follow rules to keep everyone safe. In a dorm sometimes you will have your own bathroom and shower, but sometimes there is one big bathroom for the entire floor to share. You don't have to live on campus, though. Sometimes students live at home with their parents to save money. There are a lot of exciting options and opportunities for what you will do after college. That's why it's important to start getting excited and thinking about your future now.

College Questions

Ask students to write on a sheet of paper one question they have about college, one reason college sounds exciting, and one concern they have about college. Collect the papers from the students and read some of the questions, excitements, and concerns aloud. Lead the class in a discussion about these items.

9-4 HOW TO CHOOSE A COLLEGE

Graham is a ninth grader, and he knows that he is going to college. His football coach has told him repeatedly that if he goes to a four-year college and gets his bachelor's degree he will have a lot better chance of getting a job that he will like when he's older. His coach has also told him that a bachelor's degree will help him qualify for a lot more jobs than just a high school diploma. What are some things that Graham should think about when he is choosing a college?

SUGGESTED ANSWERS

✔ A Size of the college campus

✔ B Number of students in the classes offered

✔ C Subjects offered and reputation for specialty areas

✔ D Distance from home

Summary: Graham should think about the size of the college campus, the number of students in the classes offered, the subjects offered, reputation for specialty areas, and the distance from home, among other things. Choosing a college is an important decision, but don't let it scare you. Do what Graham did and talk to your student counselor, teachers, and other adults and ask them to help you make this decision. By asking questions, Graham learned about the importance of visiting a college to see the campus. He also learned that students can talk with the admissions office to find out more about the college and figure out if a particular college might be a good fit for him. The summer before your junior year is a good time to take a road trip and visit colleges.

9-5 MORE THAN HITTING THE BOOKS

Many college courses will require you to do extensive reading, but you also could take a class in which your homework is to watch *American Idol*. True or false?

 **✓A** True   **B** False

Summary: It's true. The University of North Carolina offered a class titled "Examining *American Idol*."[42] College coursework includes a wide variety of subject matter. You have an opportunity to explore traditional subjects in depth, and you may also be introduced to contemporary issues and material such as current news and television programs. It is like no other time in an educational career—and it is the best time to take advantage of as many offerings as possible in courses called electives. College is the time when you choose your major area of study to prepare for your career, but it's also when you can take electives and take some out-of-the-ordinary classes that aren't offered in high school. Just as in your other classes, you will have homework and might need to write papers to show what you have learned in your elective coursework. College exposes you to all sorts of subjects, some you've probably never heard of. College is a great place to learn more about careers and develop skills. It pays to work on your writing and critical-thinking skills, because you will need to be able to express yourself and argue points in your papers.

The chart on the next page shows how full-time university and college students use their time on an average weekday.

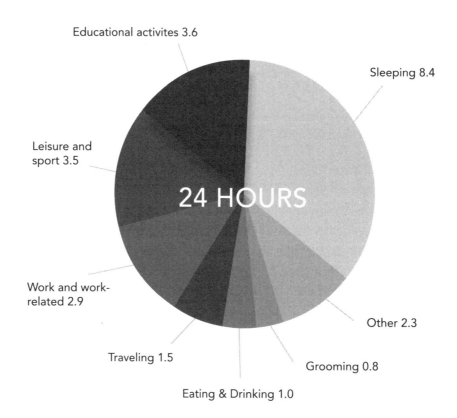

Educational activites 3.6

Sleeping 8.4

Leisure and
sport 3.5

24 HOURS

Work and work-
related 2.9

Other 2.3

Traveling 1.5

Grooming 0.8

Eating & Drinking 1.0

How College Students Spend Time . . .

Above is a chart showing the time use on an average weekday for full-time
university and college students during the traditional school year (September through May) between 2005–2009.

Source: U.S. Bureau of Labor Statistics.

SUPPLEMENTAL DISCUSSION

College Is Fun

Ask students: "Why is it important to socialize and join organizations in college?"

Suggested answers:

A. The decision to go to college should be based on the fact that education and training will give you more opportunities in the future, but in addition to your class work, you should focus on your social life. You will be able to join intramural sports teams or school-sponsored clubs, volunteer your time, participate in theater, go to a concert, or get politically active. There are many alternatives to choose from.

B. This is a time in your life when you can really learn what you like to do because you won't have authority figures telling you what to do all the time. It's all about your personal exploration and ability to make wise choices. It's another way to develop your critical-thinking skills. These experiences will help you explore interests and build and test skills. It's a chance to learn and . have fun.

C. You can learn about yourself when you meet new people from other cities, states, or countries.

CONNECTING THE DOTS

Every school day in America, public high schools lose 7,200 students. These 1.2 million dropouts will contribute less to society, are more likely to be unemployed, be involved in criminal activity, and be single parents. Those with employment will earn 37 cents for each dollar earned by an individual with more education, according to Columbia University's Teachers College.

It is the responsibility of adults (e.g. parent, teachers, community members) to reduce the dropout rate and increase the graduate rate; otherwise the income gap will continue to widen as jobs and employers require more and more education and skills. Current students not only need to graduate from high school but also need some postsecondary education or training in order to obtain jobs that pay a living wage.

Experts insist that making education relevant to students' potential career choices is important for student engagement, and dropouts agree. In a recent survey of about 500 high school dropouts, the leading reason given for dropping out is that students "don't see the connection between education and learning and their own lives and career dreams."[43]

Students begin to disengage from school in the middle grades, so it is there that we as a community of adults need to focus our efforts in helping students understand the "why" in "Why do I need to know this?" With this information, students are empowered to make good decisions regarding staying in school.

Students—and parents—are often unclear about the benefits of a technical certification or college degree. In some cases, schools and parents prepare students and tell them that they should go to college. Other times, students, especially those whose parents did not invest in postsecondary education or career preparation, are not prepared for a future that develops their own workforce potential. To compensate, educators have introduced school-to-work programs for students to recognize the connection between school learning and career development. Career pathway programs and career and technical education programs include this connection in their delivery mechanisms and mission. *Connecting the Dots Between Education, Interests, and Careers, Grades 7–10* complements this instruction and informs students about why and how to prepare for a career and/or to attend college.

The topics covered in *Connecting the Dots* help provide adults with the answer to the tormenting student question, "Why do I need to know this?" Using *Connecting the Dots*, adults can provide concrete evidence regarding why education is necessary for future success; match educational requirements with students' interests, career goals, and earnings; and inform students about college and careers. *Connecting the Dots* is a toolkit for adults to help students understand why education is important for their future happiness and success.

Connecting the Dots: Topics

1: Education: The Key to Your Future
2: More Education = Better-Paying Jobs
3: Studying, Learning, and Getting Good Grades
4: School Subjects and How They Relate to Careers
5: Ready or Not: High School, Here We Come
6: How Interests Now Spark Careers Later
7: Navigating to the Job of Your Dreams
8: There Are So Many Jobs. How Do I Decide?
9: College Life: Much More Than Studying and Classes, It's Fun!

Using extensive research, *Connecting the Dots* addresses the impact that education and training have on life outcomes, including self-sufficiency, future earnings, and happiness. It focuses student learning on critical subject areas such as school, abilities, training, college, income, and careers.

This school-to-work discussion tool helps teachers initiate and maintain a dialogue with students about career choices, filling a long-standing curricular void. *Connecting the Dots* helps students connect the dots among school, interests, abilities, training, college, and careers. It has been created at a point in our history when education and skills training beyond high school are increasingly necessary to meet the educational and skill requirements of many current and emerging careers.

REFERENCES

1   Carnevale, A. P.; Smith, N., & Strohl, J. (2010). *HELP WANTED: Projection of jobs and education requirements through 2018*. Washington, DC: Georgetown University Center on Education and the Workforce.

2   Editorial Projects in Education. (2010). Diplomas count 2010: Graduation by the numbers. *Education Week, 29*(34), 4–5.

3   Editorial Projects in Education. (2010).

4   Editorial Projects in Education. (2010).

5   Alliance for Excellent Education. (2007). The high cost of high school dropouts: What the nation pays for inadequate high schools [Press release]. Accessed January 2011, http://www.all4ed.org/files/ archive/ publications/HighCost.pdf

6   Rouse, C. E. (2005). *The labor market consequences of an inadequate education*. Prepared for the Equity Symposium The Social Costs of Inadequate Education at Teachers' College, Columbia University. Accessed June 2010, http://www.literacycooperative.org/documents/ TheLaborMarketConsequencesofanInadequateEd.pdf

7   Bureau of Labor Statistics, U.S. Department of Labor. (2010). *Occupational employment statistics*. Accessed September 2010, http:// www.bls.gov/oes/

8   Bureau of Labor Statistics, U.S. Department of Labor. (2010). Education pays... *Current Population Survey*. Accessed July 15, 2010, http:// www.bls.gov/emp/ep_chart_001.htm

9   Terpstra, A., & Clary, J. (2009). *Getting by & getting ahead: The 2009 Illinois Self-Sufficiency Standard*. Chicago: Social IMPACT Research Center.

10 Terpstra & Clary (2009).

11 Terpstra & Clary. (2009).

12 Bureau of Labor Statistics, U.S. Department of Labor. (2010). Education pays...

13 Bureau of Labor Statistics, U.S. Department of Labor. (2010). Education pays...

14 Terpstra & Clary. (2009).

15 Carnevale, Smith, & Strohl. (2010).

16 Editorial Projects in Education. (2010).

17 Carnevale, Smith, & Strohl. (2010).

18 Editorial Projects in Education. (2010).

19 U.S. Department of Labor, Bureau of Labor Statistics. (2010). Overview of the 2008-18 projections. *Occupational Outlook Handbook, 2010-11 Edition*. Accessed August 2010, http://www.bls.gov/oco/oco2003.htm

20 Bureau of Labor Statistics, U.S. Department of Labor, Office of Employment and Unemployment Statistics. (2008). *Unpublished 2008 annual average data from the Current Population Survey*. Accessed November 2010, http://nces.ed.gov/programs/digest/d09/tables/dt09_381.asp

21 Bureau of Labor Statistics, U.S. Department of Labor, Office of Employment and Unemployment Statistics. (2008).

22 Bureau of Labor Statistics, U.S. Department of Labor, Office of Employment and Unemployment Statistics. (2008).

23 Bureau of Labor Statistics, U.S. Department of Labor. (2010). *Occupational employment statistics*.

24 Bureau of Labor Statistics, U.S. Department of Labor. (2010). *Occupational employment statistics*.

25 Bureau of Labor Statistics, U.S. Department of Labor. (2010). Education pays…

26 U.S. Department of Labor, Bureau of Labor Statistics. (2010). Overview of the 2008-18 projections.

27 Child Development Institute (website). (2010). Tips for helping kids and teens with homework and study habits. Accessed January 2011, http://www.childdevelopmentinfo.com/learning/studytips.shtml

28 Carnevale, Smith, & Strohl. (2010).

29 Carnevale, Smith, & Strohl. (2010).

30 Rumberger, R., & Ah Lim, S. (2008, October). Why students drop out of school: A review of 25 years of research (Policy Brief 15). Santa Barbara: Gevirtz Graduate School of Education, California Dropout Research Project.

31 Rouse, C. E. (2005).

32 Bureau of Labor Statistics, U.S. Department of Labor. (2004). BLS release 2004-14 employment projections [Press release]. Accessed November 2007, http://www.bls.gov/news.release/pdf/ecopro.pdf

33 Hansen, R. S., & Hansen, K. (2010). What do employers really want? Top skills and values employers seek from job-seekers. *Quintessential Careers*. Accessed November 2010, http:// www.quintcareers.com/ job_skills_values.html

34 U.S. Department of Labor, Bureau of Labor Statistics. (2010). Overview of the 2008-18 projections.

35 Bureau of Labor Statistics, U.S. Department of Labor. (2010). *Occupational employment statistics*.

36 Bureau of Labor Statistics, U.S. Department of Labor. (2010). *Occupational employment statistics*.

37 Bureau of Labor Statistics, U.S. Department of Labor, Occupational and Employment Statistics. Accessed August 2010, http://data.bls. gov:8080/ oep/servlet/oep.noeted.servlet.ActionServlet

38 State Career Cluster Initiative, 2011. Accessed 2011, www.career cluster.org

39 State Career Cluster Initiative, 2011. Accessed 2011, www.career cluster.org

40 CNBC. (2009). College degrees most in demand: 2009 [National Association of Colleges and Employers]. Accessed August 2009, http://www.cnbc.com/id/29367964?slide=1

41 Knapp, L. G., Kelly-Reid, J. E., Ginder, S. A., & Miller, E. (2007). *Postsecondary institutions in the United States: Fall 2006 and degrees and other awards conferred: 2005-06* (NCES 2007-166). Washington, DC: National Center for Education Statistics, Institute of Education Sciences, U.S. Department of Education.

42 Lee, F. R. (2004, November 1). Arts, briefly: "Idol" worship. *The New York Times*. Accessed November 2007, http://query.nytimes.com/gst/ fullpage.html?res=9901E0DC1E3DF932A35752C1A9629C8B63

43 Bridgeland, J. M., Dilulio, J. J., & Burke Morrison, K. (2006). The silent epidemic: Perspectives of high school dropouts. *Civic Enterprises*. Accessed 2013, www.ignitelearning.com/pdf/TheSilentEpidemic3-06FINAL.pdf

ABOUT THE AUTHOR

Sarah M. Klerk is an expert of workforce development. In her work with Workforce Strategy Center, she helped communities develop career pathways. Prior to her work with WSC, Sarah worked at the Chicago Jobs Council to ensure access to employment and career advancement opportunities for people living in poverty. It was from Sarah's work at the W.E. Upjohn Institute for Employment Research, where she conducted research on workforce, economic, and educational development and worked with community stakeholders to improve the economy through educational and workforce development, that she gained a passion for helping students understand the value of education. This was when she decided to develop *Connecting the Dots Between Education, Interests, and Careers, Grades 7–10*, which provides adults—teachers, educators, counselors—with engaging questions to stimulate dialogue with students about the connection among education, interests, and careers. Sarah earned her Master's of Public Policy from the University of Chicago.